Comments from Readers

I enjoyed the trip. It was fascinating.

The beginning with the beer in the washer prank was hilarious reminding me of the Jackass films.

A most riveting read, well done!

I like the running commentary and how it flows.

…very entertaining.

The imagery is great and I also enjoyed the humor sprinkled throughout.

Just great.

…the part about the cowboys and your fifteen seconds of fame – then being demoted to a mechanical bull was great fun.

I really liked the irony of the kindest man you've ever met but just don't cross him.

Fascinating story.

Author's Note

Events are recalled as happened: some were expanded and changed. Identifying characteristics of some individuals have been changed, and some individuals may be composites of more than one person.

www.ravenhousepublishing.com

For information on Raven House Publishing, LLC, please send email to: ravenhousepublishing@gmail.com

Cover and back designed by Charles Pollock

ISBN-13: 978-0-9841190-0-4
ISBN-10: 0-9841190-0-0

Bar Code Legend: 978-0-9841190-0-4 – no pricing

Westbrook, ME

DRUG TRIP
CLAY HURTUBISE

Raven House Publishing, LLC

Dedications

For Mom and Dad
As he spoke,
The condom broke.
Nine months later,
I awoke.

Also...
The State Troopers of Wyoming
In the dust,
He spun around.
Their gentle guidance
A diamond found.

Never last;
In my soul,
Love he stole.
After he ate,
An ozone hole!

Forward

The adventures in this book took place in the first couple of decades of my life. The fact that I have made it another several decades is testament to a greater power. What that power is, is open to debate. Some say God, others say alcohol. Me? Still trying to figure it out, though I doubt it is something we are currently aware of.

You'll notice that two first names are assigned to me. Christopher, my given name, and Clay, my chosen name. On December 10th, 1991 I was in a nasty car accident. The intense storm had dumped six unplowed inches of heavy snow on Route 16 in North Conway, NH. The old lady traveling in the opposite direction in her land yacht saw no reason to adjust her speed and traveled through the corner sideways, across my lane. Even with four studded tires I was unable to avoid her. The sideway impact resulted in the muscles on both sides of my neck being ripped. My car was pushed toward a telephone pole guy wire, which resulted in a second impact. The combination of the two impacts created a quarter size tear on the left side of my brain and I was then a recipient of a TBI (Traumatic Brain Injury). It would be eight years before I returned to work. Christopher died in that accident, when I awoke I still had his memories, but I was starting fresh.

Short-circuit
Christopher Hurtubise
8/15/07

For some these things are explained
Spirits, ghosts, another plane.
I for one have felt these things,
Yet answers within I still must bring.

Never before would I believed,
Science background says deceived.
The brain is delicate, and complicated so,
Made it easy to explain, that I know.

Quarter size tear, but changed me how,
Brought me to the point I am now.
Pondering that which I knew so well,
Left me with time, time to dwell.

A misfire, short-circuit, or poor connection,
All names I've used
To explain my affliction.
And here I am, still amused.

Amused at myself, my thoughts, my way.
So grounded was I
So certain to stay.
Now such things I let lie.

Gray matter torn.
Who I was before?
That night I died, from whom I was born,
My new life now, no need to restore.

A baby born at thirty-one.
Experience, now what couldn't be?
The accident happened, that was done
A new me emerges, the things I'll see.

In the beginning confusion reigned.
Out of body experience, what is my name?
Head exploding, wires amiss,
Must let go of the man called Chris.

To see myself, beside myself,
Understanding and confused,
I willed myself, I willed myself,
Come together, be one, fuse.

Searing pain thru the eye,
Memories lost, least not mine.
Starting from scratch, time to buy
Born at 31, things are fine.

Monica visits more than once,
The phone she uses to announce.
Then in our kitchen, all dressed in white,
She says hello, there is no fright.

Visitors look over while we sleep,
Presence felt,
That I'll keep.
Taught me things, I have dealt.

Another ghost, in black he's dressed.
No fear though, without stress.
Even Ms Bea can see him stare,
But for her, the raise of hair.

Vision of Jamie, back at home,
As he prays he turns his neck.
Eye to eye, neither alone,
Miles apart, we connect.

This time asleep, to my side,
Others see an empty hand.
Yet in my palm his resides,
Not in this plane, I understand.

Changing now, I'm not sure why.
Perhaps the world is to blame,
Perhaps its people must learn shame.
Certainty, we cannot buy.

Twenty years after the accident I legally changed my name to Clay. The rest is for another book! So here I am, Clay, writing about a time period and events which happened to the deceased Christopher, me.

The book takes place over seven days while I was a student at the University of Wyoming. Each day comprises one chapter. During each day I recall other events that helped shaped the person I was, at least until the accident of 1991. When I write, I put the thoughts down as I remember them, so I'm often reflecting back to an earlier time then returning to my Drug Trip. The next book, Dog Trip, tells of the time from when I got my puppy, Pfizer, to the time I was knocked unconscious in the 1991 auto accident. During that time Pfizer and I would experience auto accidents and mountaineering adventures together. There was a time I saved his life, and another time he saved mine. The third installment covers the time from awakening, being told I would be a quadriplegic, to the present. The poem Short Circuit, in this book hints at what I experienced as a TBI (traumatic Brain Injury) survivor.

The third book in this series is titled Head Trip. It explains the repercussions of having part of your brain torn, and learning some basic social skills all over again.

Wyoming is a place of enchantment. The stark beauties of its land and the generous people who occupy its space have always beckoned for me to return. The police may be happy I'm gone.

Drug Trip

Day One

The snow squall encompassed everything in my world at that moment. Visibility was past tense. The wind was wicked, constantly shifting direction and changing in intensity. The motor was starting to sputter as gas was being consumed far faster than ever before. When it stalled, I guided my Yamaha 650 motorcycle to the side of the road as safely as possible.

To this day I feel responsible for another students' death. It was an accident but haunts me still. Being alone on a cold wintry stretch of Wyoming road made me think of him. Just last week, while writing, I think he visited me. Though even now my ripped brain still won't allow me to fully accept the presence of ghosts. Being analytical in nature I tend to think of ghosts as an image within our own mind, like a projector gone wild. The image is real to me, but is it 'real' in everyday sense? Why my Soft Coated Wheaton terrier, Ms. Bea, chases one, well, I can't explain that. Death and life go hand in hand, but having to be the one to place a DNR (Do Not Resuscitate) order on one of your parents is tough. Being involved with the DNR for your sister, tougher still. Later in life I would be able to save lives, but it never makes up for the one I feel I cost. Until last week, the ghost that I see, other than the one in the foreword, is always the same; a thin tall man wearing a hat. Picture a crisp dark shadow of a man on the pavement during a bright day, and then pull the shadow up so it is standing upright. That is how 'Fred' appears; he is not transparent. Now I think that if ghosts do exist, this new ghost that I see is the student. Like Fred, he never gives off negative energy and somehow I am comforted by their presence. It is as if they are looking out for me. I tried to save one life, but failed.

No other Maine-iacs were near by. This lonesome bit of interstate 80, high on the plains of Wyoming, is home of fierce winds and lonely hearts. Originally I had expected to make it to Rawlins before refueling. My hands were freezing and I found it necessary to take off the bulky down mittens my roommate, Ray, had loaned me. Now I could use the spare gallon of gas, which was strapped to the back of the chrome sissy-bar. Originally I had thought the spare gas would never be used, certainly not within the first two hours of the trip. In the past I had made the trip to Rawlins with fuel to spare, but the wind that day was intense even by Wyoming standards.

Most of my college class was on a drug trip. Literally. The ones with financial holdings of at least a few hundred dollars had all gone to Illinois for the week to visit drug companies. The University of Wyoming Pharmacy College sponsored the trip every two years. The idea was to familiarize the students with the drug manufacturing process. As I was cash strapped like a Mormon hooker, I sought another adventure. One of the reasons for attending school in Wyoming was so I would be able to explore more of the good ole USA. Before moving to college in 1975, I had never ventured farther west than the eastern side of Vermont. As a paperboy for the Portland Evening Express (now defunct), I was one of hundreds competing for a free trip to the brand new Walt Disney World in Florida. For every new customer you got a point, and you could also get points by selling magazine subscriptions to your current customers, or anyone with cash. My blue eyeballs were on a shiny new ten-speed bike. Ten-speeds were all the rage; until then most kids had either a single speed or a heavy, slow three speed. A few days before the contest ended my boss from the newspaper called and asked if I had a preference: a couple smaller prizes or one big prize. My head was spinning; this must mean I got the bike! After delivering the Sunday papers and buying my family the traditional box of assorted Dunkin Donuts, I sat down on my parents new black leather and brass studded couch, and felt my heart sink as I spotted an article on the winners of the newspaper contest. Imagine my surprise when I found out I had won the trip to Florida for selling the most new subscriptions! So I managed to go south, but I stayed in my own time zone until I left for college. A motorcycle trip to California sounded, at least that morning, like a grand idea. Cheap, exciting, and on my own terms, it was my kind of road trip.

When I was in high school I bought a tired 1968 U.S. Postal van from the government for six hundred dollars. It was right hand drive with sliding side doors. Though it had only 23 thousand miles, it required a fair amount of work. Even with the blue stripe painted over, people would approach me and hand me their mail. Never did find any cash. Kidding. Being eighteen I thought this was a pretty cool vehicle. Within a few weeks I had installed gold

wool carpeting on the floor and on the plywood bench seats, which I had had made from scrap wood. Cork was glued to the walls to quiet the interior and a large cooler, just for soda of course, was fixed to the floor. It was my first paint job, and I did it in my parent's driveway. Green, sticky beechnuts would fall on it as I tried to paint. Squirrels would jump on the van, going for the beechnuts, which had fallen moments earlier.

Initially I was going to make it look like a UPS truck but have the logo say OOPS. Either that or put the logo of "the Miracle Chair Co., 'If it's a good chair, it's a miracle'" It ended up brown with a beige stripe, and of course, squirrel footprints on the roof. This was the vehicle for my first road trip. Fuel economy was horrendous. Gas had skyrocketed that year to over $0.50 per gallon. In the city it got 15 mpg, on the highway it was more like 10mpg. Only had 2,322 miles to go. Driving through Pennsylvania, (why do residents there all say they are from 'P A'? In Maine we don't say we are from 'M E') was trying. The van simply wasn't equipped to maintain speed over those hills. Often I found myself in the far right lane with the semi trucks, doing 45mph, emergency flashers flashing, heart racing. About mid way through 'P A', the fan belt broke. Luckily my Dad had prepared me for this and I was able to change it and move on. What I didn't realize was that he never finished the exhaust, which was right next to the brake line. The first night I parked in a massive lot near a large mall in Toledo, Ohio. The black rain was flooding the parking lot. It was surprising to me that it was pretty much the same as the mall back home. Didn't know there was more than one 'Spencer's. For the first time I realized that America was homogenizing.

The next day, while slow, went pretty smoothly. Rows and rows of corn, then the gentle green hills of Iowa. At a free campsite in Small Ville, Iowa I parked next to a huge, shiny new Airstream. The quintessential old lady was the sole occupant. Her husband had died and she sold everything they had accumulated over their 35 years together, and planned to live out her life in the Airstream. Not one to turn down an offer of cake, I went inside. It was luxurious. Beautiful detailed woodwork, tile, carpet; it had more luxuries than our home in Maine. This trip was teaching me more than any school course ever could, and interacting with complete strangers helped build my confidence in myself. As I traveled from state to state I learned that while accents vary and local customs could be colorful, people are people, no matter where you plant yourself. If you treat others with respect, half the battle of getting along is won. Perhaps this says more about DNA than any scientific paper. Scientist need to get out of the lab.

Next was Nebraska, where initially the lack of trees was overwhelming. Over time this feeling would change, and now I find it comforting. When I thought it was 3:00 PM, I pulled over into a small rest stop, took off my t-shirt and sneakers and sprawled out on the lush green grass. Occasionally I'd open my eyes and notice other tourist looking at me strangely. While no one would mistake me for an Adonis, neither am I homely, and though I was in good shape, certainly no reason to stare. After a half hour of soaking up the rays I glanced behind and saw a sign; "Do not walk on the grass – rattlesnakes". That not only explained the looks I got but motivated me to get going. The crowd was explained by the time. It was my first trip outside of Eastern Standard Time and by overhearing some kids realized it was actually noontime, and this the best picnic area for miles. Nebraska is so flat you could put a brick on the gas pedal and go in back to sleep, and then wake occasionally to check on the steering. Mile after mile of unchanging scenery. Just like the openness, the tranquil, open vistas would become a welcome sight. Then the landscape changes dramatically at the border. A hill!

Wyoming is windy. One explanation that Wyomingites like is that it is windy because Utah blows and Nebraska sucks. Utah and Nebraska have their own thoughts on it. A rancher from Nebraska told me that the slogan for Wyoming is "Where men are men and sheep are nervous" He also said, while looking at some sheep, that Velcro, was invented in Wyoming. Who you gonna believe? After passing through Cheyenne, I-80 approaches its highest point at the Abe Lincoln Memorial. It was just after here that I lost my brakes. Exhaust fumes had corroded the main brake line. The road was under construction at the time and I was driving on a dirt road between two eighteen wheelers. Over the course of the next few miles the descent is over 1,200 vertical feet. The emergency lever was on the right side, but my right hand was injured from a fall off my unicycle just two weeks prior. There I was, driving down the hill, reaching over with my left hand to use the emergency lever, at night, wondering if I'd make it the last few miles! At the bottom of the hill things got better. By reaching over and using the emergency brake and keeping the transmission in low, I was able to get into town. Not sure of which way to go, I ended at the intersection of 3rd and Grand. The nearby Cowboy Bar was just shutting down and I was parked at the intersection. It was 1:00AM. A herd of Cowboys had been released and they were streaming toward my dusty van. Several of them slapped their palms against the wide area of the van and hooted and hollered. Swear to God, if my brakes had worked I would have turned around and gone home. Non-stop.

A month before my drug trip I had bought my friend's motorcycle from him. His new wife wanted a freezer, so the bike had to go. Don't know which lasted longer, the freezer or the marriage. Two hundred dollars was a lot of money to me, but basically I was buying a four-cylinder freezer. During school I held a variety of jobs; ran a kitchen at a frat house, fed rats, mice and guinea pigs, washed UPS trucks, worked in the oil fields, and worked at a hospital. With such

a deal on the bike I managed to scrape up the cash. Some of the best money I've ever spent. The bike was in great shape and I took it everywhere. At the time I belonged to Big Brothers; I was the big brother. My little brother, Mike, who fancied pet rats, would go with me on the bike to the rugged mountains for hikes.

We would drive forty miles to hike a half hour and then return home, him to his little apartment with his mom and brother, me to

my dark little bedroom at the apartment. The bike was remarkably reliable. On one trip that I took alone to Fort Collins, Colorado, the chain felt loose. I'd tighten the chain but it would loosen up after 20 or 30 miles. It didn't dawn on me that there could be a problem. Not on my bike. On the return trip I was on a hilly section of Route 237 when the engine started racing wildly and the bike started slowing. It took some time to hitch back to Laramie, and then retrieve the bike. The mechanic in Laramie was shocked. The front sprocket was worn completely down. He didn't know how I had managed to ruin it as completely as I had, (one of my many hidden talents!) and he worked with motocross bikers all the time. He wanted the old sprocket, but I kept it as a paperweight. Mike thought it was cool and wished he had been there. Great kid.

In Laramie it was a cold October morning back in 1977 when I loaded the bike and took off with no map or clear destination. In the backpack, strapped to the sissy bar, were a tent, down mittens, 35mm camera and other borrowed items. The bike, sleeping bag, and a few clothes were mine. To prepare for the trip I had changed the oil and installed a new rear Michelin, tire and tube. When I wasn't riding the bike I would store it in the hallway of Ray's and my dark apartment. The only problem was it was a basement apartment and I would ride the bike down the narrow cement stairs, hit the brakes, and leave it parked outside our door.

Getting back out was always a challenge, but hey, I was twenty! As an afterthought I had strapped a one-gallon can of gas to the back - smart, eh? I thought so. Just wish everything had made it back.

That spare gallon of gas in the red and yellow metal container would be enough to get me to Rawlins, where I planned to say hi to my adopted parents. My birth parents lived in Maine, 2,322 miles away. They supported my college and adventures as best they could, but it was work-study programs, odd jobs and a lot of student loans that got me through the expense. The trusty Yamaha started right back up. There was no traffic. The snow squall was subsiding and after a torturous half hour I emerged into glorious sunlight. The Maxsons were surprised to see me in a way, and not in another! After we had a quick lunch in their beautiful home I was back on the road with a Willie Nelson song in my head, Don't Fence Me In.

The summer before I didn't have enough money for gas to get home, as my Dad's Chrysler 300 drank gas like an Irish man does beer, so I drove to Rawlins in hope of finding a job. Had no idea what I might do, but I had heard that Rawlins was booming and needed all the help they could get. That first night I slept in my Dad's green 1968 Chrysler 300 and ate at a quickie mart that offered frozen leather burgers you could nuke. Yummy. That left me with less than five dollars and a tank low on gas. Next door was a liquor mart, but that would have to wait. The following day I hooked up with a friend, Jerry, from Laramie, and he was able to put me up for a week. That first night, as I lay on the couch, I grabbed a pencil and a paper bag and wrote:

missing

Home, home, let me know you're still there,
Tell me, how are my friends, and all I love dear?
Home, home, you know I still care,
God, I wish I were near - I wish I were there.

Home, home, I never thought I'd miss you like this.
It is almost too much to bear.
Home, home, please send me a kiss,
Just something which we both can share.

Home, home, it's where I truly belong.
Where I can laugh, sing and cry, where I hope I will die.
Oh please, please, take me back home.

Years later my Mom was at her antique mahogany desk and asked me if I wanted to see something. Sure. She opened the bottom drawer, retrieved a small stack of paper, and then handed me the poem, 'Missing', that I had written to her over a dozen years earlier. Mom.

Jerry had a wild streak in him. He took me for a ride in his green 1968 Volvo 'The Saint' car and we streaked along at 100mph on a dusty old two-lane road. The first night with him the tequila flowed too freely and he got his musket rifle out. "Hey, see that hotel sign across the street?" "Yah". "Watch". A deafening boom echoed off the walls of the cozy apartment and a hole opened up on the neon sign across the street. A dozen years later I returned to Rawlins and just had to check; sure enough the hole was still there. Jerry called the parents of a mutual friend who was out of town for the summer and they agreed to put me up. Mr. Frank Maxson was an intimidating teddy bear of a man.

Kinder soul didn't exist, just don't cross him. On my first morning there, at 7:00am, Mr. Maxson told me to get my lazy ass up and meet him at the car. He drove me to a paving company where I was promptly hired. My job would be to operate machinery I had only seen before. Later I would move into Mr. Maxson's parents' house, as his nephew, Kleeber, was staying there while Frank's mother lived in a nearby nursing home. The Maxson's made me part of their large family. They included me in everything they did, including chores. Week ends at Seminoe reservoir, meals at the local restaurants, installing storm windows, and drinks at the family table. Knowing I was from Maine, they couldn't resist the chance to serve me Rocky Mountain Oysters! The way the whole family accepted me and helped me is one of the reasons I love Wyoming.

How they taught me to Water ski.

How I water skied.

One night grand-mother Maxson sat me down in her room and explained that I would have to pay rent. Mow the small lawn and ten cents a month. At the end of the summer I got an uncirculated dime and typed a thank you note to her. It was in a walnut frame and the dime for the last month took cen-ter stage. She hung it up in her room where it stayed till

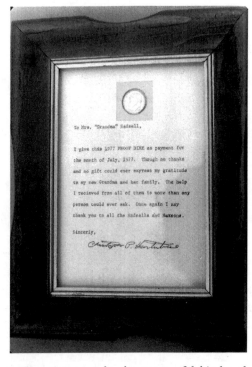

she died. The people in Wyoming proved to be resourceful, kind, and hard working. Just don't piss them off!

Of course, me being a smart mouth college kid I was bound to piss off someone. After work a few of us would kick back and drink a substantial amount of beer. On one particular night we had the not so bright idea of driving around Rawlins while we consumed the hops. The car we were in was a big old four door American boat, spe-cial class. The driver and a passenger were in front. In the back we had a tall, skinny, passed out cowboy on my right, myself with two cases of beer on my lap in the middle, and another worker on the left. Not sure who had the brainstorm, but we emptied the window washer then refilled it with beer. We then turned the window washers sideways so we could spray unsuspecting folks with suds. After a few minutes of this we hit on the grand idea of going up to one of the many drive up liquor stores. The poor unsuspecting worker opens the drive up window while the driver of American Boat hits the window wash button. Dead on. The attendant was shaking his head while asking us what we wanted. Well, we wanted to know why he just stood there while getting soaked with beer. Didn't know that many swear words could be spoken so fast. After we drove off another brilliant idea was brought up. Bet the attendant wouldn't recognize the car if we pulled in with passenger widow to his side. He didn't. He also didn't take nearly as long to start swearing. God knows what possessed us, but in a few minutes we just had to try it again. The third time was eerie. All the lights went out as we approached the building and the attendant ducked out of sight. UH OH. We decided enough of that and took off. We were at a red light when the now very drunk cowboy in the front jumps out and starts pounding on the roof of the car in front of us. He was slurring that he wanted the hat from the car driver. We coaxed the cowboy back with more beer. Then we turned left and were second in line at a red light. The light turns green, but the driver doesn't move. We were honking and hollering the best we could. We were oblivious to our surroundings, but not for long. Right out of a Bruce Willis movie a swarm of police cars moved in from all directions. Front, back, both sides. All four lanes blocked off. Caught. Within moments each window had a .44 caliber handgun, hammer pulled back, pointed into the vehicle. Sobering. The guys in front got out right away. The door to my left was broken, the cowboy to my right passed out. The officer is screaming at me to get out and I'm trying desperately to wake the cowboy. When he does wake he found himself looking straight down the barrel of the pistol. "Huh?" We got him out and then we were all placed along side the car, hands on the roof, feet spread, and hearts racing. The pistols are holstered then the questions start. All very good questions. Just tough to sound insightful when you're inebriated. The driver was, amazingly, sober enough to drive. We were all given warnings and told to go home. We did. We just didn't stay there. Cowboy number one had a van, which we promptly jumped in, with beer, and drove off to down some suds. The following weekend we decided to walk around town and go bar hopping so as to stay out of trouble. Problem is we still got drunk. On the way home we had to pass the police station. The road was under construction. There was a huge highway construction sign just down the street, with flashing yellow lights and reflective tape. It all added up. We heaved and hoed and dragged the mighty sign and placed it sideways so it completely blocked the entrance to the police station. The following weekends we stayed home and drank without getting into, or causing, trouble.

After the visit I was back on the road and heading toward Rock Springs; a tough town filled with hard workingmen and cash earning women. The road through Rock Springs is beautiful. Tunnels cut through the bedrock yield open vistas and deep blue sky. At the time it was a throw back to the Wild West of yesterday. I vaguely remember an episode on 60 Minutes where a reporter was stabbed during filming, gripping footage. It was different from the rest of Wyoming. Lot of transient folks there and a harder edge to everything. In Rock Springs there had been a lot of mining and occasionally a sinkhole would open up and cleanse the land.

My goal was to make it as far into Utah as I could get. After leaving Rock Springs the ride was great. Warm, sunny, and no wind. Shortly before reaching the Bonneville Salt Flats, I was cruising merrily along at about 70mph, down hill, the sun setting before my eyes, and all was right with the world. BANG! My new Michelin rear tube blew apart. The explosion caused the bike to bounce violently up and down and from side to side.

Perhaps it was a good thing I had tried bareback bronco riding just a month earlier. This wild hair had attacked me and I developed a hankering for bronco riding. Not knowing how to get started, I drove to the edge of town and looked for a home that had horses. Not seeing my action as inappropriate probably helped me. At the house I walked up and knocked on the door. A lovely woman answered; "Yes?" "Hi, I'm Chris Hurtubise and I'm from Portland, Maine and I'd like to learn how to bronco ride". Her eyes momentarily got wide as saucers. She didn't see any hidden cameras and she must have figured out I was serious. At that point she invited me in, sat me down at the kitchen table and cooked me a thick steak. She asked me a lot of questions then wrote ten names down on a piece of paper. "Take this to the OK Corral tomorrow morning and tell them I sent you." As much as I love Maine, I can't imagine some twenty year old knocking on some door and asking to be taught to ski. At least not without making headlines. At the OK Corral the sky was bright, deep blue, and not a cloud in sight. When I went inside the rustic bar section of the corral, my eyes needed a few minutes to adjust while all the cowboys took a look at the greenhorn. There was a tall lanky cowboy standing off to the side and I approached him with the list. All the names were visible to him. Starting with the first name I asked if he knew him. "Yes". "Is he here?" "No". When we got to the tenth and final name once again I asked if he knew him, "Yes". "Is he here?" "Yes". "May I speak with him?" "You are". With a gleam in his eyes and a faint smile emerging, he asked a cowboy at the bar to lend me his spurs and glove, both very personal items for a cowboy. Without hesitating he said he would. The tall cowboy then looked at his watch and said he'd have me on a horse in fifteen minutes. He paused, looked at his watch again and stated he'd have me off the horse in fifteen minutes and four seconds. I made it five seconds. Greenhorn Chris was the morning entertainment, with all the cowboys sitting on the bullpen fence ready for the show. At the end they all came up to me and told me stories of their beginning. The tall cowboy then said if I saw his truck outside I'd be more than welcome to stop in and he'd throw me up on the mechanical bull. Turned out that tall cowboy was the ex world champion. A buddy at the frat didn't believe me. One day we were driving by the OK Coral and I spotted the truck. When we went into the coral I was greeted by a loud "Hello, Mr. Hurtubise". My friend was shocked. Moments later my butt was sore.

The Yamaha was my new bull. Clenched my fist around the controls as hard as I could. The driver of the car passing me slowed to watch the spectacle. He had some kids with him and while their noses were squished against the window they were pointing and shouting toward me. Problem was his slowing meant there was no place for the 18-wheeler behind me to go. The truck driver laid on his horn and I could hear all eighteen tires of his truck screeching. While my rear view mirrors were bouncing all over, I did make out the very large grill that consumed the whole field of view and decided it was time to pull over. When I got the bike to the gravel covered shoulder it flipped, tumbling through the air with me grasping its handlebars. Somersaulting with Yamaha. Slammed against the guardrail with my head at an awkward angle, the bike lay across my chest and the handlebar pinned my right hand to the broken pavement. The backpack had broken loose and had gone air borne over the guardrail and down the dusty hill. It took me a few minutes to absorb the situation. Parts of me hurt, bad, but most everything seemed to work. Gas was trickling out of the gas tank, down my pebble imbedded leather jacket and onto the hot exhaust pipe. My hand was still pinned and

I couldn't budge from the guardrail. It would be a year before my right hand worked normally again. Traffic flowed by. Ah, humanity, who needs New York City? When other's lives were at stake I always had that famous burst of energy. Just a year prior I was with Ray in his car. We were at a light on the West side of Laramie. A gorgeous, tall young woman with flowing blond hair was approaching the intersection from the left side of the car. She was walking two handsome, proud golden retrievers with fur that flowed like her hair. As she stepped onto the street a quick moving car from our right side made a swift left turn. The first dog was run over by the beat up car and scarcely a moment later the beautiful lady was airborne and landed with a heavy 'thump' in front of Ray's car. The second dog had bounced off the hood and was thrown back into the middle of the intersection. Without pause, I unlocked the door, ripping the door lock in half. In seconds I was at her side, assuring her everything would be OK. I lied. Luckily an ambulance just happened to be returning to the hospital and before I had finished draping my jacket over her, help had arrived. The astounding part was yet to come. Two weeks after the accident the careless driver called me at the frat house. He asked me if I would state that the woman had been running across the street. My reply was calm, I stated that I would definitely give a statement and would call the police just as soon as I hung up. Yet here I was on I-80, unable to help myself. My mind was running through memories as I anticipated dying a fiery, gruesome death soon. After several minutes, which felt like an eternity, a gray van pulled up behind me. It was the elderly couple I had talked with at the last gas station. They were rambling the countryside with no particular destination. They had asked me that if I made it to San Francisco to call their son and tell him that his folks were doing just fine. Of course I had agreed. Now they were on I-80, two thin elderly folks, probably no more than a pound of calcium between them, pulling with all their might to lift the bike off me. The ordeal exhausted the woman and she went to rest in the van. The man stayed with me. As I sat on the cold gray steel guardrail I trembled and cried as I tried to explain what had happened. His soothing voice and demeanor helped relax me. It took a while but we got the rear wheel off and they took me twenty miles down the road to the nearest gas station. The attendant couldn't believe what had happened and fixed the tire for free. My saviors bought me a burger, chips and a soda at the counter, and then they drove me back to my bike. He positioned his van so its headlights shone on my bike and I could work safely. When everything was put back together they followed me to their turnoff point. For years we exchanged letters and Christmas cards. We waved goodbye, then parted ways and I began to look for a place to camp.

It still amazes me to this day how cold people can be. Well before the time of cell phones, no one but the old folks thought I was worth the few minutes out of their busy day to lend a hand. Oh, they may take a quick picture, but not even a police officer showed up, leading me to believe all those kind souls were to busy to use the gadget of the day, the CB radio. A part of me wishes that I could return the favor to some of those folks one day, but for whatever reason, I'm not wired that way. Thirty years later nothing has changed. Just a year ago I was attacked on a busy street by a raged man trying to kill me, but no one intervened.

This is a desolate area of Utah. When I left sight of the old folks it was dark, the air crisp and the sky was full of stars. I was going just at the speed limit. A shiny pickup truck pulled up along side of me. The driver looked over at me with cold, emotionless eyes, then without warning rammed me sideways as hard as he could. Once again I'm air borne. This landing was harder. The heel of my right boot ripped off, the bike tumbled and I lie in the dirt gasping for air.

Mentally I check off the basics... legs move, arms move, not feeling blood gushing out... Then, still lying in the dirt, my heart pounding, I hear a vehicle pull up and I pray it isn't the pickup driver. Why was I attacked? What would provoke a perfect stranger to try and kill another human? Was it the bike? Would this have happened if I were driving a pickup with a gun rack in the back window? This trip

could not provide me with an answer. While people are much the same the world over, they are the same in both good and bad traits. If this were the cold truck driver, certainly I would be killed. Would my body be found? Would my parents ever find out? No, it's a man who was traveling the opposite way and saw the attack. Swear words flying out of his mouth as he describes to me what he saw. He helps me up and then the two of us lift my battered bike up. The right mirror is all twisted, the front forks are leaking hydraulic fluid and the Yamaha is no longer nice and shiny, yet it starts right back up. After a few minutes I assure him I'm OK, though I ached horribly all over, and I thank him profusely. He is hesitant to leave me. This looks as fine an area to camp as any, I told him. After he pulled away I drove

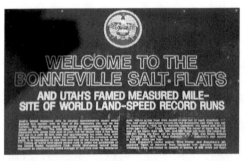

down the steep embankment and parked the bike. It was set at idle so I could use the headlamp for light. When the borrowed tent was partly assembled, the bike's kickstand sunk into the salt and the bike fell on its' right side. The throttle opened full, the engine screaming. Realizing that I didn't want an engine part to mate with my body, I backed away just as the engine died. The tent was up as far as I was willing to take it. With the sleeping bag unrolled I crawled inside and quickly drifted off to sleep.

Day Two

Blaring car horns woke me up. Evidently you're not supposed to camp on the Bonneville Salt Flats, and my orange tent must have bothered some drivers. When I poked my head out the half erected tent my first thought was to return to Wyoming and recuperate. My second thought was frig that. It had to get better! Have you heard the one about the two boys who each find themselves in a horse stall neck high full of manure? Boy 1 is swearing and hollering to get out, keeps slipping on the stall sides and falling back into the manure. Boy 2 starts digging frantically and exclaims; "S★★★, with all this manure, there must be a horse around here somewhere". I'm boy 2.

With substantial effort I was able to get the bike back up. Seemed every bone and muscle in my weary body ached. There was no rush to get it loaded, but as the sun rose and the warmth filled my spirit I got energized and ready to continue my adventure. The bike wouldn't start. The one and only fuse had blown. The spare sat in its little holder, shattered, mocking me.

The previous summer I worked in the dusty oil fields of Wyoming and Utah. While there were a lot of rigs, it was hard finding one we felt comfortable with. At night we would drive over the foot deep, mud back roads to the drill sites. Couldn't stop, for there would be no way out if you lost momentum, and staying on the road was a constant challenge. At one site we interviewed at we needed the help of the full crew to get us moving again, and then the road ate my muffler. The United States was in the middle of yet another gas crisis and when we finally found work our job was to shut down productive oil fields. Go figure. It was a hazardous job but it paid well; no pun intended. Certain areas of nearby oil fields were off limits due to toxic gases, it was imperative to be cautious. Venture into the wrong field and oil wouldn't be the only thing underground. The rig I worked on was a collapsible oilrig, the immense four front wheels turned and the hundred foot tower, which when in the collapsed position and lowered, now a mere sixty feet long, onto the truck still overhung the top of the cab by a dozen or more feet. The vehicle was extremely top heavy and yet fairly easy to drive, just real difficult to stop! It was an automatic and I had to wear ear protection when I drove it. A mere six-inch drop off (at the shoulder of the road) would be enough to flip it. As I had a chauffeur license I was one of the few able to drive it, legally at least. Once while driving it on a two-lane freeway I spotted a state trooper heading my way, red light flashing and passing a line of traffic. As soon as he spotted me he pulled into his lane, let me by, then pulled back out.

My first day on the job I started at 6:00 PM to work the 12-hour night shift. It took an hour and a half, often driving the four-door crew truck at over 100mph on dirt roads, to reach the well site. Around midnight I was standing at the base of the rig when the derrick hand (the derrick hand is the man who works about ? of the way up the derrick and handles the pipe) yelled "Heads up". Not sure of what to do, I stood still as I listened to a clanging getting progressively louder. An eighty pound, four foot long piece of steel buried itself in the soft sand between my feet. The derrick hand raced down the rig and grabbed me and asked if I was O.K. I was, but unlike James Bond, I was shaken and stirred.

Some folks say I have bad luck, but I see it the other way around, I'm extremely lucky. Sometimes stupid, but also lucky. Like when I was first working in the kitchen of the frat house we developed a bizarre game. Catch the Knife. The idea was to toss the large carving knife, sharpened weekly, from one end of the commercial kitchen to the other and catch it by the stainless steel handle. Stupid. Divots in the floor and door attested to multiple failed attempts. Lunch cleanup was just wrapping up one day when Jim came in through the swinging oak doors and hollered 'heads up'. Well, my head was in the refrigerator and by the time I spun around it was too late, I caught the knife, not by the handle, but by the ten-inch blade. Four fingers on my right hand were sliced at the second joint, bleeding profusely. When I rushed to the sink and turned on the water I spilled a bottle of ammonia over my fresh wounds. It was the scream heard around the campus. A dozen butterfly joints and a lot of bandages later and I was back in business. Lucky.

Every morning at the oilrig the same joke was played out. As the job was intense, dirty, and dangerous, everyone was always on full alert. Without fail someone would stop what they were doing and go; "Shhh. Did you hear that?" "What?" "Oh nothing, just the crack of dawn". We fell for it every day. At the end of our shift we would bolt for home. Housing in Rawlins at the time was scarce and my roommate and I were paying $550 per month for a two room, ant infested shack. We were lucky. Lots of folks were living in tents. Our landlady would often ask me over to fix some trivial problem while her voluptuous breasts struggled to stay within the insufficient blouse. She wanted more than her indoor plumbing fixed and I wanted to stay alive when her enormous merchant marine husband returned home.

At one point we worked two straight weeks of twelve-hour days combined with three hours of high-speed travel. That left just nine hours to get cleaned up, eat, sleep, get up and prepare lunch. Whew. About half way into our work marathon we had an argument about what day of the week it was. Along a mostly barren stretch of road was a small, run-down filling station. Our driver slammed on the brakes and pulled over allowing me to jump out. Gasping, looking like hell warmed over, I ran into the station and asked; "What day of the week is it?" "What?" "What day of the week is it?" "Sunday". "Thanks". We all had it wrong.

Crewmembers didn't last long. Various things would make them leave; family, injury, better job, or in the case of the crew next to us, death. It was important to be mentally prepared for the unexpected and when my roommate and I had been looking for work we first met the crew chief one well over. While working, the whole crew was smoking grass. We declined, the marijuana and the job. The crew chief next to us wanted to save some time, and in his altered state of mind made a critical error, he released one guy wire to let a truck through quicker. While we watched in astonishment the whole rig collapsed, killing two workers. Nearest hospital was a half-hour helicopter flight away. On a less tragic accident it took us three hours to get our co-worker with a crushed foot to a hospital.

Three of us lasted a month and were then assigned to a different rig. The crew chief looked at his list, looked at me and said; "Mark, you're the derrick hand". "I'm Chris". "Chris, you're the new derrick hand". "I don't know what to do". "You'll figure it out". My training consisted of how to put on a safety harness, (they loaned me one for the day then had me go shell out $65 for my own), and a warning that should a well 'come-in' I should jump on the special guy wire and slide down to terra firma. My work platform was a narrow strip of perforated steel that looked like a sadist attempt at a diving board. As the pipe came out of the hole I was to unclamp it, push the lift mechanism out of the way, and guide it into one of the metal 'fingers' beside me. Turned out I was pretty good at it. So good that the crew chief thought it would be great fund to grease the handles. That resulted in my losing my grip, the pipe falling the wrong way, a stack of sixty foot pipe shifting, my getting thrown into a corner with pipe entangling me and my safety harness keeping me from falling. Later in my life I would survive several falls, always by sheer luck, but that was a tough one. The crew chief was startled and sincerely apologetic. The crew chief kept me awash in beer for a few weeks, his way of saying 'sorry'. It was shortly after that incident when we took half a day to scrub the rig from stem to stern with diesel fuel to clean it up. It really looked sharp, for a few hours. "She's going to blow", I heard as the rig began to shake. Within seconds a powerful jet of crude oil and noxious fumes were spewing to about 120 feet into the air, inches away from me. The oilrig uses two twelve-cylinder engines for power. The fumes from the oil are highly flammable. Instantly the rig and I were covered in crude. Without thinking I grabbed my Buck knife and sliced through the steel safety cable. Unable to make it to the guy wire slide I went down the ladder with the oil still gushing inches in front of me. The rest of the crew was standing far away as they were expecting an explosion. In about fifteen minutes a helicopter arrived with a crew of well, (honest, no pun intended) trained workers who, within hours, capped the errant well. Thoughts of my folks entered my head, and while I would return to the rig the next day, my appreciation of my folks and all I held dear grew immensely.

When I was young my Dad would take my sister and me to Old Orchard Beach. At the time it was Maine's version of Coney Island, only filled with lovely French women and fat thong wearing French men. My Dad had spent a lot of time as a child here. His mother loved to move, claiming it was the Native American Indian in her, so he got to live in various neighborhoods. He always pointed out the place where he saw a deaf man get run over by a train. Deaf man had been walking in the direction of travel for the train, which in those days passenger trains sped along at 60mph. My Dad and his friends yelled at Deaf man, but it was over very quickly. Only now do I doubt the event. Most likely it was a terrifying story meant to scare some sense into me. He loved to explain how things worked. When words wouldn't be sufficient he used tools, like when he had me hold the lawnmower's spark plug and cap while he gave the engine a good yank. "That's why you don't touch wires!", he laughed as I got a shock from the wire. So it seemed odd that he didn't answer me

when I pointed at a display window full of dildos and asked; "What are those?" OOB, as it is affectionately called, was popular for its Pier fries, pizza, amusement area, and uncommon gifts. The crown jewel was the merry-go-round. Hand carved horses, lions and other beast painstakingly carved in Germany. Meticulously painted and maintained, it was truly a sight to behold. One night a fuse had blown so the operator replaced it with a penny. Not positive, but I'm pretty sure they found the penny after all the ashes cooled down.

Penniless, I sought alternative ways to fix the bike. After removing the shattered fuse I used electrical tape and joined the two connections together. Presto! It was running like a top. Leaking hydraulic fluid, scratched and dented, but running great. The salt was softer than it looked and the embankment to I-80 is steep and tall. Did it grow overnight? My first two attempts to get back on the road were futile; the front tire would sink into the embankment. Seeing no way onto the highway for miles, I drove out into the salt flats and turned around. After the previous night I wasn't too keen on the human race. A half-mile lead provided ample time to build up speed, which I did. Drove straight onto the embankment like a wild man and at the crest of the hill I popped a wheelie and drove straight into two lanes of traffic with cars and trucks scattering to get out of my way. Horns were blaring, tires squealing and a huge grin was on my face. Alive.

Breakfast usually consisted of something nutritious from the gas station. Whoopie Pies, difficult to find in Wyoming, were always a favorite, that and a Coke. Thirty years later the only difference is now I drink DIET Coke, (cancels out the calories from the Whoopie Pie).

Once when I was young, around 10 or 11, my Mom made a batch of whoopee pies. Hers were the best. Not huge, just great chocolate and the best filling oozing out of the side, calling for your tongue to lick it. That night we had company, and company brought a daughter. Daughter, evidently, had already consumed a lifetime worth of whoopee pies. Our Mom was adamant that we stay in the living room and visit with our company. Porkie took off for the kitchen. Monica and I looked at each other with trepidation. Mom had left the large platter in the middle of the Formica kitchen table stacked high with all of her scrumptious whoopee pies. Please God, please, let there be some left over. After the visit Monica and I dashed into the kitchen. While the delicious aroma lingered, not a crumb remained. Not that I ever would wish diabetes on anyone, but come on! Not even a crumb!

Day two was going by well. Counting down the miles to get out of Utah was a joy. At college I had several friends who were Mormons. For the life of me I can't grasp that religion, course Roman Catholic, how I was raised, is no better. One of my pharmacy buddies was always trying to get me to convert. He must have needed points to win a toaster or something. Coke was one of my main food groups, but he could never have any. Then one day a big wig in the Mormon Church bought a huge share of the Pepsi Company. Mormons are required to donate ten percent of their earnings to the church. The very next night the leader of the Mormon Church had a vision from God, it was OK to drink Pepsi in limited amounts, but not Coke. The church received a lot of ridicule over this and shortly after the leader had another vision from God. It was OK to drink any soda, in small quantities, and even coffee and tea! Hallelujah!

Later I learned that there are two types of Mormons, much like any religion. Group one adheres to the bylaws as best they can. Group two, the 'Jack Mormons', are more liberal in the practice of their faith. One New Year's Eve I went to a party hosted by some Jack Mormons. They can be a wild crowd! Alcohol flowed freely and everyone danced up a storm. It was a helluva party. On the way home, Jack Mormon thought he'd show us his idea of fun. He drove on the opposite side of the road, which was divided by a median strip, for several miles, which caused most of us to sober up pretty quick.

Miles melted by and soon I was entering Reno. Gambling isn't my thing, at least not with my hard earned cash. One look at the casino and I asked, how do they afford this? My money comes way too hard to drop into a one-arm bandit. So while I enjoyed the bright lights, I drove right on thru. The California border was approaching but both the bike and my stomach needed refueling. There was a burger joint with massive glass windows facing an empty parking lot. No time to be fussy. After setting my scratched helmet on the table a waitress approached me. "So, like, you the one driving the bike?" "Yes". "Where you going?" " Well, no clear destination, but right now I want to drive to the end of I-80". "You, like, in school or something?" "Yes, I attend the University of Wyoming" "Is that like, in Illinois?" "No, it's in the state of Wyoming" "Oh, well, like, I don't know my geography all that well"

After I ate the average burger and fries I asked her, yes I should have known better, if there was any place cheap to stay nearby. She directed me to a place just over the California border. At the time California had border guards, just like entering another country. The Land of Oz. The large border guard who greeted me was going to confiscate my small orange, but he eventually let me through with it. He actually knew the place where I was heading and gave me detailed instructions. The driveway to the long two story white motel was narrow, tree lined, and dirt. As I drove down a man with a rifle stepped into the driveway. Weird, I didn't think it was hunting season. After driving around him several more stepped onto the driveway and blocked my way. "Why is everyone wearing a bullet proof vest?", I wondered. The headhunter approached me and asked what I wanted, why a room of course. He told me to look elsewhere. "Thanks, but this looks fine" When the rifle was pointed at my bike he flashed his badge. Shouldn't he have done that first? Then everything came into view; there were cops everywhere, all with rifles pointed at the motel. More special unit vehicles than you would see in a double episode of CSI. Time to turn around. Though I was tired I decided to head for the coast. Drove over some cold mountains but I was too tired and it was too dark to see anything. At least no snow. The guns had unnerved me and while I should have pulled over and camped, thoughts of the rifles and the man who pushed me off the road the previous night kept me moving. It was past midnight when I made it to San Francisco. First order of business was to find a pay-phone. Son was either not in or not awake, but I left a message that his folks were not only fine but they helped me in a time of crisis. Probably the weirdest message he ever got. Next it was time to find a motel. There was one that had a window right next to the sidewalk. It was expensive, so I declined, but a passing man, dressed all in black leather, even a black hat, offered me the other side of his bed. I declined that too. Down the road was a policeman, were the YMCA guys out at that time? Anyway, I stopped the cop and asked if it was OK to camp on the beach. At first he looked at me like I was nuts,

then noting that I was from Wyoming he warmed up and gave me directions to an area I could camp at. Bit further than I wanted to go as I was as tired as day old beer. "It's on a bluff, so make sure you don't drive too far". Sage wisdom. The bluff was deserted and as the night was warm I didn't use the tent, just unrolled the sleeping bag beside the bike and fell asleep under the stars while listening to the waves pound the walls of the cliff. When the morning sun woke me up I took a look around. Spectacular sunrise, incredible view. The bike looked weird. Was it because I was lying down? No, more to it than that… My stupidity level is the highest among mankind. I had slept on the side of the kickstand. Did Utah teach me nothing? The bike was perilously close to tipping over. That would have woken me up! As I needed another hour of sleep, I moved my gear to other side of the bike and quickly dozed off again. Safely.

Day Three

This day was full of promise. For just what I would learn later. Considering we were both so battered, both the Yamaha and I, things felt pretty good. All my joints moved, some better than others, and the bike started right up. If all went right I would stay at Ron's house. Ron is an old friend who moved into my quiet neighborhood from Canada when we were in junior high.

At the time my family lived on the corner of Woodford and Nevens streets. His family; mom, sister, brother and two aunts, moved into a brown duplex three houses down, when Maine was still full of stately elm trees. It would be with Ron that I would experience some of my first 'close calls'. Certainly not the first one I remember, and being a Catholic 'accident' isn't included. My first close call was with my sister Monica, my brother Leo, and my mom. Monica and I were always close. We removed belly button lint together. Twins born years apart. Close even after she died, but that would be years down the road. The night she died I held her through her final breath. It may be wishful thinking, but at the time it appeared as she was on her last breath, to recognize me, then her eyes went dark and lifeless. The drive home from Boston was brutal. Never had I felt so alone, so insignificant. Though it has been years since she died, it still brings tears to my eyes and I must pause typing.

Obviously I'm no poet, but writing is cathartic for me and I couldn't sleep that night until I put this down on paper;

I LOST MY SISTER...

DEDICATED TO MONICA E. TAES
BY CHRISTOPHER P. HURTUBISE

I lost my sister,
Oh silly me.
Seems only moments ago I kissed her,
where can she be?

It's a big world out there,
that much I know.
She's the one with tousled hair,
and oh, she hates the snow.

So while you're looking here or there,
give me a call if you think it's she.
I'll just keep looking for that tousled hair,
cause I lost my sister, oh silly me.

To reach back in time now long gone,
I remember from early on.
We were always close, my sister and me,
she was even there when I sliced my knee.

From hiking with Dad on a rainy day,
to a crazy bike trip , or a mountain stay.
We bonded with adventures and time on our side,
knowing each other so, we had nothing to hide.

So where is that sister,
that sister of mine?
How far can she go in desert or snow,
when we have the love, the love that we know?

There she is, oh silly me.
She's waiting there...don't you see.
Deep in my heart, my thoughts, my mind,
she's moved from her body, into mine.

 That fine sunny summer day we were playing chase in and outside
of the house. The house was built at the close of the 19th century
and had many fine details. One detail was the swinging fifteen glass
paneled door in the hallway between the kitchen and bathroom. The
glass was heavy and thick, only semitransparent, and was textured
with heavy vertical lines. Fast on the heels of Monica, she swung left
at the end of the front hallway and headed toward the large yellow
kitchen. As she barreled through she reached back and swung the
glass door in a successful attempt to stall me. Instinctively I raised my
left hand to push against the door so I could continue my fruitless
pursuit. The forces of nature being what they are, my hand lost the
battle with the door. The center panel of glass and my left wrist made
a scarring impact. Shards of thick glass exploded into the kitchen
while deep red vital fluid gushed out from my wrist. Graceful arch-
es of blood painted the kitchen walls. Wa. Instant tears as piercing
pain let me know I was in big trouble. Monica, knowing the seriousness of the situation, quickly ran out to get Leo who was mowing

our small lawn. He immediately let go of the lawnmower, which lacking any safety gear, not only rolled down our little hill but also proceeded to run down the entire length of Nevens St. It just happened that as he started for the side door our Mom was just stepping off the city bus one house away. She arrived as blood was dripping down walls, I was screaming, Monica was crying, and Leo was applying pressure to my wounds at the antique porcelain kitchen sink. Mom had been exposed too much worse early on in her life and I remember how quickly, yet calmly, she called the operator for help. Within minutes a burly policeman was in our kitchen, gently yet quickly, picking me up and rushing me out to his squad car. The ride to the hospital was fun. The single roof light was on and the siren was on full alert. We zoomed through traffic and ran red lights. Whee! As we went up the steep hill toward Maine Medical Center the loss of blood took it's toll and I passed out. To this day my wrist looks like I need to be on suicide watch.

Kitchens weren't always a place of physical pain; there could also be emotional pain as well. When I was very young my folks took the lot of us to visit one of our aunts. She had a tendency to get a little hot headed, but it was always quickly resolved without much drama. As often the case, the kitchen became the main draw while the other rooms lay vacant. For whatever reason I had gone to the sink area while the rest of my immediate family was on the other side of the Formica covered Kitchen Island. My aunt, whom I normally thought as loud and fun was on one side of me, became angry with my uncle who stood on my other side. The argument had to do with an older topic and I didn't understand the ferocious of my aunt's anger. She grabbed the nearest weapon; a large heavy handled butcher knife, and swung wildly at my uncle. The image of the shiny blade swooshing past my terrified face is permanently etched into my retinas. She didn't even see me, nor realize how close she had come to giving me a split personality, when she raised the knife again. My mom, one to seldom raise her voice, screamed at my aunt to stop. Mom then charged her way toward me, scooped me up and announced that we were leaving. My aunt and uncle were upset about the turn of events, apologized profusely, but it would be a long time before we visited there again.

At the same kitchen where I played Catch the Knife, I learned a lot about human nature. One frat member was against my hiring a Latino for help. The frat member was also a friend of mine and he also worked in the kitchen. The Latino turned out not only to be a better worker, but a better friend. He was use to the discrimination, though that didn't make it either OK or acceptable. In the end I would have to choose one of the two workers to keep. For me it was no contest, I needed a worker and that was who I kept. Eventually the frat worker came around and understood my position, even apologizing to the Latino. It seemed a lot of the college students carried baggage packed by their family and friends. In college one of the hardest things to do is to learn what to keep and what to throw away. My friend learned to throw away some heavy baggage and he was a better person for it. Having to hire friends to keep the kitchen running also meant I was always being tested. My friends would like to push me to see how much they could get away with. One day I was carrying a large pot of fresh tomato soup. Otis, my current roommate, (we shared a large basement room that we outfitted with weathered pine boards, taken from snow fences, and tacky mirrors) kept coming in the kitchen and horsing around. At the second warning I told him there would be consequences if he so much as poked his head back in the kitchen. Normally he was a jeans and t-shirt kind of guy, but that day he had an interview and he was in his Sunday best. Silly boy came back into the busy kitchen. Without so much as a word I simply dumped the gallons of warm soup over his head. Then I made him clean it up or face more consequences. He never tested me again. At the time I was nineteen and running a kitchen that supplied three meals a day to almost forty members. With little prior experience it proved to be a challenge. It was also my responsibility to keep the budget under control, yet these were finicky eaters. Slowly over the semester I was able to reduce the whole milk to 1%, and even then at times I would mix powdered milk and cut it with the 1% to make the dollars stretch. Cereal was another large cost and the guys simply wouldn't eat the generic corn flakes. Finally I smartened up and saved the empty boxes of Kellogg's and would refill them with the generic. This says more about society than just fooling a few college frat boys.

There on Route 1, in sunny California, I was low on gas, figuratively, and the first order of business was to find a filling station. A dollar a gallon! Holy Cow! If this doesn't stop people from driving nothing will! If you haven't traveled Route 1 from San Francisco to L.A. you owe it to yourself to get out there and do it. Amazing drive. That particular day traffic was light, the sun was out in full intensity, the air was warm and dry and I was in heaven. Never had I driven a motorcycle so hard. Zen. Never would I drive a bike that way again. Sanity. Sparks would fly when the foot pegs scraped the ground as I cornered as hard and fast as possible. It was as if machine and man had merged. While I thought I was being extremely observant, the truth is I got lost in the moment. The yellow sign notifying drivers of a hairpin turn escaped my ocular input. At the crux of the turn there is a small paved overlook. It was packed with cars and people milling about, soaking up rays, gazing out at the magnificent views, and taking pictures. Their serenity was rudely interrupted when I stood up, initially to jump off the back of the bike but when the backpack stopped me I stepped heavily on the rear brake and grasped the front brake lever with all my might. Not enough. The ole Yamaha and I skidded between parked cars and were headed toward starting a new sport, motorcycle hang gliding. Fortunately a large rock was parked at the edge of the seemingly thousand-foot cliff. The front tire hit square into the boulder at about 20mph. The rear of the motorcycle quickly lifted high into the air and as I grasped the handlebars I felt the bike teeter. I was doing a handstand; my butt and feet had left the bike and were pointed toward heaven. After I viewed the waves pounding the coastline far below, the bike and I fell rearward toward safety. A man ran up to me and grasped me by my shoulders and shook me hard as he said; "Are you all right?" Slowly I lifted the visor on my helmet, looked at the man and said, "Nice view", then promptly restarted the bike and drove off. A few minutes down the road the full impact of what had just occurred sunk in, I pulled over and trembled as I looked back at the cliff, still full with people, many pointing in my direction.

To be alive today is nothing short of a miracle. Many, not alive at least, don't match my level of stupidity and carelessness. As I've gotten older I have slowed down, but back in those days I might have set a record for stupid acts, unfortunately none are recorded or I could put 'Jackass' out of business. Two years prior I had my Dad's green Chrysler 300, a beast of a car. Jim, a high school buddy, and I found out that if you were doing a 100mph in it and punched the gas you'd get pinned to the seat, even on a snow packed covered highway. Fast car, slow brain. So one day I was returning to Laramie with some friends, in that same green Chrysler 300, after a trip to Vedauwoo, a rocky area outside of town near the Lincoln Monument. Just before entering Laramie the highway narrowed and became two lanes wide, and I was stuck behind a lethargic eighteen-wheeler. Having had enough of going slow, 50mph, I punched it. As I pulled the green monster out to pass the long truck a Wyoming State Trooper was fast approaching from the opposite direction. Not being enough room for all three vehicles, the trooper pulled over and spun out of control in the dark red dirt. Clouds of dust appeared and visible contact with the trooper was lost as I thought "Oh oh". Kudos must be given to the State of Wyoming, for they must train their troopers exceptionally well. He had that car, dust and all, back under control in seconds. The highway patrol car was behind me before I hit the town line; it's siren screaming, red strobe light flashing, and my pulse rate soaring. As I was then doing the speed limit I cranked the window down I waved for him to pass. No luck. When he approached my window I couldn't tell which was redder, the strobe light or his face. "Young man, don't you know what a red light

means?" "Well, in Maine it's for the fire department and we pull over to let them pass, police are blue." He looks at me for a short time then took my license with him back to his car.

My friends were counting their cash to see if they had enough for bail. "Next time be more careful passing and always stop for police as soon as possible". He handed my license back to me and even wished me a good day. I love Wyoming.

There would be more interaction with the Wyoming State Troopers, and I hold them in the highest regard. More professional and courteous troopers aren't likely to exist. The following summer I worked in Rawlins, and while I drank a lot in those days I never drank and drove. My father had been adamant on that and on wearing a seat belt.

When I was about ten years old I was in our kitchen with our mom. For whatever reason we were both looking down the hill on Woodford's street when an accident occurred. A fast moving sedan coming at it from the opposite direction struck a white four door Rambler. The impact was violent, ripping the drivers door completely off the car. The Rambler then struck a utility pole and came to a stop. My mom called the operator and I ran out of the house to see if I could help. The windshield had a large outward dent, all cracked and covered in blood. The driver was conscious, but bleeding from his forehead. After assuring me that he was OK, he wasn't, he asked if I would make him a promise. "Sure". As he spoke he said, "Take this quarter only if you promise me to always wear your seatbelt". " I promise". He then got out of the car and walked behind the church across the street. Never found out what became of him. I've kept my promise. The Rambler had seven miles on it. My father let me drink before I hit the legal age of 18, as long as I promised not to drive. I promised.

In Rawlins, not knowing my way from my friend's apartment to my place I started to turn one way then changed direction. This must have looked suspicious to the watchful trooper. This state trooper car not only had the fancy strobe light bar on top, but also spotlights on either side of the car. After I had passed the first line of sobriety test he had me face the car then recite the alphabet, first forward then backwards. With a puzzled look on his face he informed me that I kept missing the same letter. After two more attempts he asked if I truly knew the alphabet. I quickly recited the Greek alphabet, forward and backwards, and stated if I knew that I ought to know the English alphabet. "Well are you nervous or something?" I said you stand here and face all these lights while talking to a trooper and see how you do. He turned around and had his partner kill the strobe and spot lights. "OK, one more time, slowly" "P, Q, Ahr" "There, you keep forgetting 'R'!" "No I don't, it's Ahr" "Geez, you're from Maine, is that how you talk there?" "Ayuh" We both had a good laugh and he escorted me home. I love Wyoming.

There is another Wyoming State Trooper event I'd like to share. It was only a few weeks prior to my drug trip. While I loved Wyoming from the moment I got there, at times it was extremely difficult to be nineteen and over two thousand miles from home. On one particular night I drove to one of my favorite spots off I-80. It's a back road that rises high above the interstate. There is a small parking area where you can pull over and enjoy the views of Vedauwoo and the Abe Lincoln Memorial. The hum of traffic rises up but is muffled by the scrub pine trees, which due to the constant wind have branches on only one side. There is a split rail fence about fifty feet from the edge. The Chrysler was parked facing I-80, engine and lights off. The air was crisp and cool as I sat on the rustic fence and thought about life. The lights of a car illuminated my little sanctuary of the rest area, and then the car drove off. In about ten minutes the lights returned. A trooper parked his car some distance away, gently closed his door then walked toward me, and sat on the fence about ten feet away. Neither of us spoke. After several minutes he quietly asked if everything was OK. "Yeah". "Miss home?" "Yeah". "Need to talk about anything?" "No, I just like to come up here and escape for awhile". "So do I, if you ever need to talk about anything I'm leaving my card on the fence". "Thanks". It would be an honor for me to meet that man today and tell him how his kindness and generosity made such an impression on me.

Back on the bike my attention was more focused on the signs and I dropped my speed. It remained a beautiful drive, just a bit more sane. The day was still young, as was I. The road became a bit straighter, and then the number of cars rose dramatically as I approached Santa Barbara. Long before I was even a thought my folks had lived there. They had met during WWII. My mom and her sisters ran an underground railroad in Belgium.

Mom's Story

The cold dark machine gun barrel was pressed into her slender throat once again. Arrogant, powerful, and soulless, the Nazi questioned one of the four sisters; "Are you carrying papers?" yet again. The sisters were an integral part of the Resistance. Only teenagers, their youthful innocence robbed by the war machine, they played an important role in the lives of Jews and stranded Americans.

The dark red brick home and local pub was situated at an important crossroads in Veltem, Belgium, during the Second World War. While the sisters and their parents went about their daily lives, bombs were being sent overhead and into their village. Rumors floated amongst the lips of neighbors that there were resistance fighters right in their own backyards. Most were joyous at the thought, but there lurked others eager to turn in their neighbors for a favor from the occupying force. Word reached the sister's home that the Nazis would be doing a search, looking for a particular pub described to them by a treacherous informant. Their father was also a carpenter. He worked through that day and into the next morning. The old pub didn't exist anymore, in its place was a pub, but not the one described. The Nazi search proved fruitless.

Time came for one of the sisters to be 'questioned'. She spent her endless days without leave in a closet too small to sit in, too dark to see, and too far removed from her innocence. The Nazis learned nothing. The other sisters were more determined. The papers flowed.

Being too crucial to leave alone, the Nazis occupied the sister's home, forcing the family into a few rooms. While searching for the resistance and occupying the crutch pin of that same resistance, Jews and Americans were ferried right under the stench full noses of the Nazi war machine. It was all too blatant to be recognized. The ruthless destruction of the sisters' home and country went on. Father died. Having been denied medical attention, he suffered and was buried without a headstone in the local church's grassy yard.

Liberation. So much damage on so many levels. Multiple continents united in a fight for freedom. Dad meets Mom. Mom's violated home is now occupied by the determined Americans. Nazi papers are found. They had scheduled the sister's family for elimination in ten days. Close. Now powerful American antiaircraft machine guns are placed in the basement of the sisters home. In the dead of night, piercing lights would be aimed at the drone of the engines from retuning Nazi fighter planes. The house would rattle under the fire of the machine guns. Sisters would shake. Cry. Pray. Night turned into day.

Four years later my parents were in a double wedding ceremony. Two of the sisters were saying vows that wouldn't be broken. Decades later, my dear sister would perish from cancer, like her mom had just a few years earlier. In the bright family room of a large hospital, I met with my sister's oncologist. We talked about family. Roots. His father had barely escaped from the Nazi regime. It was through the tireless effort of a few sisters in a small Belgium village.

Dad had joined the army shortly after Pearl Harbor was bombed. At first his mother didn't want him to go, but as the seriousness of the event took hold, she gave up her fight to keep him in secluded Maine. Grandmother, being who she was, sold all of my Dad's possessions while he was fighting: as she didn't expect him to return.

His first tour of duty had him on the front lines. Seldom did he talk of this, but one night when I was in high school and the house was quiet he talked at length about his time in the military. As he described the events, his mood changed and I could notice how he was less with me and more with his old cronies from the army.

There came a time when the sergeant asked for volunteers for a dangerous mission. My Dad and his buddy volunteered, but no one else did. Their squad had been hit hard the week previous, and many of my Dad's friends were dead. The Sergeant excused my Dad and his buddy from the trip and sent the remaining eighteen soldiers to the mission. Two returned. After that the Sergeant redeployed my Dad to the heavy artillery division. Dad didn't do well there and while he had a strong sense to do the right thing, he felt he wasn't being utilized to the best of his abilities. The Sergeant agreed and arranged to have him be a driver for The Red Ball Express, a fuel delivery division that brought supplies to the tanks and heavy equipment as they forged their way across Europe. It wasn't long before Dad became the lead driver and he told me how the trucks had the doors removed so the drivers could jump out easier if the truck was hit. He told me harrowing stories of driving through sniper fire, speeding along at night with almost no lights, and loosing the breaks to a double semi tractor filled with gasoline as he sped down a mountain pass and through a small French town.

It was common for him to be near the front lines and they lost many trucks to enemy fire. When the tanks began rolling into Belgium, he was there. That was how he and Mom met: he a tired truck driver and her an Underground Railroad facilitator. After the war they communicated by letter for four years. After the double wedding ceremony they found their way back to the United States: my Mom never to return to her war torn village.

After she settled in Maine, her sister would send her Belgium magazines almost monthly. All I did was look at the pictures and comics. If memory serves me right, the Smurfs made their appearance in those magazines long before they became popular here in the states. Another comic was Lucky Luke, a cowboy faster than his own shadow. She got a kick out of this and we would often look at it together while she translated the text for me. A couple years ago I was

thinking of getting a tattoo in memory of my Mom, but couldn't decide on what to have inked. Low and behold, I was watching the BBC channel and the Belgium Tourism department was running and ad and for just a few seconds it featured Lucky Luke. It took some tracking on the World Wide Web, but finally I found some old comics for sale on eBay. Lucky Luke and his unfortunate shadow are now permanently inked on my left arm.

Mom was also a fighter. It wasn't until I was in High School did I learn of her inner strength. It was in my freshman year, if memory serves me right, that I came in for dinner after helping my Dad and brother hang a deer from the garage so the crimson blood could drain out before taking it to the butcher. She had received three letters from Belgium and Leo stated that was an omen of bad luck. How right he was: grandmother had died. Mom wept for the relative I had never met; yet she still prepared dinner.

About a year later she showed her strength and fighter's will in a tougher battle. She was a voracious reader and had learned about self-examination for breast cancer long before pink ribbons popularized it. She had felt a lump in her right breast, and as hard as it was for her to visit a doctor, she scheduled a visit with the family doctor. The doctor told her it was nothing to worry about, so initially she let it go. As she read more and more, she regained concern and made another appointment six months after the first one. Just to appease her, the doctor sent her to be examined at the hospital. To this day I remember walking into our kitchen after school and seeing my mother standing alone, silently crying. She took me into the living room and explained to me what was happening and that she would be in the local hospital for at least a week. When I asked if she might die she told me no, she would fight this with all her strength and come home. She was right, and after she had her breast removed, she returned home. The good news would not last even through the rest of that school year. The cancer had spread and now her left breast and lymph nodes were infected. This time it was life or death, and we didn't know what to expect: the stakes had been raised. She was in the large hospital for several weeks, but she pulled through. She had been through a double mastectomy and had her upper lymph nodes removed. She was in a lot of pain, but never once did I hear her complain. Years later we would discuss it more intimately, and she said how it was a brutal battle for her. My father, she said, showed more emotion and support than she imagined possible: this from a man who rarely told he loved me. Mom may have not showed emotion as easily as others, but I never doubted her love. Her life as a teenager had forced her to hide emotion as a matter of survival. While it may have been difficult to break out of survival mode, she was never cold, or emotionless, just more reserved. It would be years before cancer would rear its ugly again, and it wouldn't be the last time. Not to brag, but I think my Mom was the best ever. Just typing this makes my eyes well up with tears.

So I had two reasons to visit Santa Barbara, one to see the first place my folks lived and secondly to visit Ron. With about forty miles left to go for the day I was traveling on a six lane interstate, again downhill and around a corner, when the rear tire went flat. A lot less dramatic this time, no bucking bull, no loud bang, and no eighteen-wheeler screeching behind me. Under full control I pulled the Yamaha over to the shoulder and pulled completely off the highway, the bike perpendicular to the road. While cars and trucks buzzed by I started the process of removing the rear wheel. A motorcyclist that was passing made a sudden stop, skidding sideways and creating a red cloud of dust that temporarily hid my view of his aged Harley Davidson bike and himself. As I sat in disbelief, he got off the bike, meandered over toward me, and sat on the hillside behind me. "Flat tire, huh?" "Yeah". It may be a wild guess, but I think he is related to the Nevada waitress. He didn't speak again till I had the wheel off. Again I felt trepidation and fear. Were more bikers going to show up and rob me? Was I going to make it to Santa Barbara today? With the wheel off the Yamaha the stranger stood up and asked if I needed a ride. "Sure" He told me wait while he started his bike. After a dozen or so kicks the Harley was leaking a fair amount of oil. "You have an oil leak" "A Harley has to leak oil in order to run right. Cops are always hassling me about it at rest stops. They don't understand" Then, with the umpteenth kick, the bike roared to life. "Hop on" That was easier said than done. As I climbed onto the 'bitch seat', my knees were near my chin, the remarkably small back support dug into me, and when I grasped my wheel I felt completely insecure. We took off like a rocket. While I try not to swear I believe my exact words were "Holy Shit". It was about twelve miles, or ten minutes, to the nearest station, but who's counting? We made quite the pair, me in a traditional leather jacket, helmet and gloves, Harley Man in jean jacket complete with gang emblem, dark blue wool hat with long greasy yellow hair and he wore no eye or hand protection.

A grand entrance into the filling station completed the gray hair event. The mechanic literally dropped what he was doing and came over to me. Evidently Harley Man was well known, or at least had a larger than life reputation. As I removed my helmet the tall mechanic asked what the problem was. "Flat tire" "No problem" With sincere gratitude I turned and thanked my oil laden driver. "No problem" He refused any gas money and said he was happy to help a fellow motorcyclist. All this stunned the mechanic who hurried the job and said "No charge" Wow! Even more amazing, Harley Man stuck around and offered me a ride back. What the hell, at least I knew what to expect.

The return ride was as quick if not quicker than the first trip. Harley Man seemed to forget that I was on his bike, grasping my wheel with clenched fist, and becoming very religious. The highway had three lanes in either direction, a large median that had steep embankments on both sides, and lots of traffic. We were in the far right, northbound lane and I could see my trusty Yamaha off in the distant. Closer and closer, yet Harley man didn't change lanes. Perhaps he was going to find an exit further up? His head bobbed up and down after I tapped his shoulder and pointed toward my bike. Without so much as a glance behind him he turned Harley quickly toward Yamaha and cut across all the traffic, down the embankment, across the middle then up the opposite embankment. Pulse rate soaring, sweat streaming, I gripped my wheel and prayed aloud. He didn't slow down for opposing traffic, just cut across all three lanes, hit the brakes, turned the wheel and executed a perfect slide up to my bike. Shit. Wish I could handle a bike like that!

We talked a bit after I got my wheel back on. On the outside he was about the toughest, meanest looking specimen of a human that I had ever seen. Inside he was all teddy bear. When I asked why he didn't wear a helmet his expression changed. It was as though he was another person and he replied, "Because I like the feeling of the air". His bike was severely chopped, it had extra long front forks. When I mentioned this to him he said at one time it was chopped even more so. He was doing 60mph and ran into a parked car. His injuries were so severe that he had an artificial eye socket. When he took his wool hat off and parted his long greasy yellow hair I could see something was clearly wrong with his cranium. Part of his skull was smashed so extensively that it was replaced with a metal plate, so he said. This compelled me to ask: " and you still don't wear a helmet?" With this response his composure not only changed, but his voice took on a softer tone; "No, I like the feeling of the air" Truly I could not judge a person by his/her appearance. The man in the pickup truck who purposely ran me off the road looked like Joe Neighbor, but possessed an evil heart. The bike looked like evil incarnated, but to me was an angel.

There was no way I could handle my bike as well as my angel could, but I had gotten pretty good with cars. That green monster Chrysler 300 of my father proved a hoot on the dirt roads of Vedauwoo. Nothing beats rear wheel drive for handling. It wasn't uncommon for me to exceed 60mph on a single lane, twisty, potholed dirt mountain road, at night. Adrenaline rush. My passengers were generally too drunk to care, though I was always sober. The rear end of the beast would slide out on the red dirt and I would punch it, pulling it back in line and going even faster. If there are such things as guiding angels, mine was working overtime.

Dad had bought the Chrysler when I was a junior in high school. Cheverus High School was an all male college preparatory school. When I was a senior I bought the postal van. The van lacked a lock on the driver side, but that didn't bother me. The lack of a lock proved very popular with my classmates who used it as a hideout to drink and smoke in. The principal approached me one day and confronted me about my van. My smartass reply was that since I lost my scholarship for my senior year (simply a dirty trick by the school-as if a student would change schools for the fourth and final year) I couldn't afford to fix it. The following day I was called to the principal's office and asked if I knew that my van was parked out on the field at the top of a hill. No, I hadn't parked it there, but I was told to move it or lose parking privileges. There was half a joint tucked under my dash, and I didn't even smoke!

Fellow classmates found it hilarious that my van was at the edge. Of course, they found other ways to tease me, or should I say have fun with me. Often I was bored with school, as it didn't provide much of a challenge, so along with a couple friends we took up drinking during school hours. At breakfast time we would zoom down to the agency liquor store and buy the cheapest vodka available. Age was never a barrier and once we became 'regulars', buying liquor became all the easier. A flask fit well in my sport coat pocket. Screwdrivers were the breakfast of choice. One day I had a few too many and it was my turn to give my report in AP Biology. As I spoke the teacher had his back to the class so Gabe, another school buddy, thought it was the appropriate time to light my blazer on fire. While other students frantically 'put me out', I kept speaking about sharks and the teacher was never the wiser. This only prompted me to drink more, and by study hall time I was completely inebriated. Kevin, whom I had known from first grade, had me sit on the floor behind a desk then up ended a waste paper basket over my head. Ahh, it felt good. Dark, quiet. Seeing that it didn't bother me he decided that more extreme measures were warranted. He grabbed me by the tie, dragged my sorry ass down the hall, past classes in session, and deposited my body in front of the oak library door, which swung out. The old Jesuit in charge of the library was a bit hard of hearing, so Kevin banged incessantly on the door, and then hid. Jesuit couldn't make out the problem, but he would have none of it. He ambled off to the other entrance. Kevin quickly re-appeared and grabbed my knotted tie once again. Dragged back past the same classes, only at a higher velocity. When Kevin got to the concrete and metal stairs he didn't hesitate, just pulled me all the way down and out the door. Now propped up against a wall with the warm sun washing over me, I passed out. When classes were let out Kevin came back and woke me up.

That wasn't my first nor last drinking at school or a school function. When I was a sophomore Sam and I planned to have a few before being picked up by some friends for a basketball game. The most logical place for us to drink was outside the large bay window of my parent's house, right where my Dad was parked in his black leather chair. The shotgun was upstairs. We kept quiet and polished off the two six packs of Naraganset pounders. Sam was peeing on the sidewalk when our ride showed up. He sat in the back and I was in the front red bench seat. We were running a bit late and the driver was going a bit fast in his pristine black 57 Chevy. The snow proved too much and on a small hill we lost traction and found ourselves spinning when we hit the snow bank. Just as the car had finished turning 360 degrees and was about to hit a utility pole sideways, the trusty Chevy emerged back on the road, pointing forward, but stalled. Quickly we were back on the road with no lesson learned. While on the turnpike I felt the need for fresh air and unable to manipulate the complicated window crank so I simply opened the door. Falling sideways my face was bobbing only inches from the pavement when Sam grabbed my coat and yanked me back in. Undeterred, I tried again but this time I opened the door just as we were a wee bit too close to a guardrail. My head hit the window as the door slammed shut and I slept the rest of the way to the game.

The cold air invigorated me. The group of us headed up to the top section of the foldaway bleachers, as high up as we could go. With the need to pee taking precedent over any other thought, I stood up and proceeded to fall literally head over heels all the way down until I slammed into the back of my home room teacher, one of the few non Jesuit teachers at school. He looked at me and told me to get the hell out of the building, and he told the approaching Jesuits it was just an accident and I was fine. As the car was locked I fell asleep in the snow until the game was over. At the start of the following fall semesters, Mr. Malia would always end with; "And I never want to see any of you as drunk as I saw Mr. Hurtubise".

The road to Ron's house was busy but without drama. He greeted me warmly, though I must have not only been a sore sight, I hadn't showered in days. We could no longer have our favorite meal, pepperoni pizza and beer, as Ron had fallen victim to Californitis and became a vegetarian. Augh. Couldn't even have ice cream, Holy Cow! If god had intended us to be vegetarians why do kittens taste so good?

When we were in high school, both Ron and I were bicycle mechanics for a local shop. He never told me how he got the financing, but while still a senior at Deering High School he opened Maine

Cycle. The space he had rented was a former laundry mat. We did a lot of the work ourselves, including demolishing a forty foot long concrete platform. The fact that we were doing this on a Sunday morning with a jackhammer didn't go over well with the preacher in the church across the street. We may have gone to tell him, but the large gothic stone church had " No Trespassing" signs all around it's perimeter.

It was 1974 and the U.S. was entering another gas crisis. My dad ran a Chevron station and he had two sets of flags, one green meaning he had gas to sell, and the other red meaning he was out. It may be time for me to dig those out. People were fed up with large American boats and were changing to smaller cars, giving Japan the entire boost it needed, as our answer was the Chevy Nova and Ford Pinto. Bikes quickly became the cause de jour and bike paths started popping up everywhere. Bike business was booming.

Ron had managed to get a CCM contract and started off with about fifty bikes. We stored them in the basement and assembled them upstairs. Using an assembled ten-speed as a pattern, I had done a

cutout in plywood, which separated the sales area from the repair area and also allowed a bike to be on display. Genius.

What wasn't genius was when I figured I could hook up the large 220V air conditioner myself. The one golden rule of one wire at a time saved my butt from getting fried, as I accidentally did it with the power still on. Kinda like the time my sister Monica and I went and watched a large fire. We could see the intense flames from a half-mile away, licking at the stars, and we could feel the sizzling heat from across the fire hose strewn street. As she looked at me quizzically, she asked what I was holding onto, as I had climbed a tree for a better view. A branch, of course. She said I might want to take another look. It was a thick black power line.

When we worked at Maine Cycle the source of our caloric intake was the Quality Shop, where we could get a nine-inch pepperoni pizza for eighty-five cents. During the day we would drink Dr. Pepper or Coke, at night our drink of choice was Foster's Lager. To successfully rocket a Foster's was a feat deserving of another Fosters. In case you haven't done it, to rocket a beer you put a hole in the bottom, cover it with your finger, give the can a mild shake, open the can upside down and have the contents wash down your throat in seconds. Fun, but messy. Burp. If we weren't working on bikes, we were riding them. A century, (one hundred mile), bike trip first thing Sunday morning had become habit. We'd be done by 1:00PM and have the rest of the day to screw around. We were also fond of riding our bikes at midnight to OOB then returned home after getting a slice of pie from Bill's Pizza. On one particular night we were on a narrow road under construction. As a large truck started to pass us a car quickly approached us from the opposite direction. All four of us were ditched in the salty marshland. This provided us with lots of banter on the way home. As I had lost my water bottle in the spill I informed the group I was going to pull into a restaurant's parking lot so I could get a soda from the vending machine. Little did I know that the first entrance was gravel. With a slide worthy of a million dollar baseball player, the bike and I made a beautiful skid across the driveway, creating a nice gray cloud in the foggy air. "Where's Lawyer?" "Lawyer?" "Over here" They were a merciless bunch and all were doubled over in laughter as I plucked various sized stones from my legs and arms. Years earlier Ron had trouble collecting from an ornery customer on his evening paper route. Later the man received a call from a perturbed "Lawyer" representing Ron's family. The customer paid and I gained a nickname.

So that night Ron had his vegan meal while I chowed down on a meatball sub with extra cheese. At least he still drank Fosters' beer. He filled me in on what it was like for him to be on his own, so far from home. He has remained there to this day and I can't say I blame him. We were each experiencing the same feelings and emotions, just different settings. Later in life a riff would come between him and his brother, much as one developed between one brother and myself. It is easy for a non-family member to pass judgment and proclaim how such a thing would never happen in their family. How blood is thicker than water and nothing should disrupt it. Maybe something should. It is a simple statistic that shows most violent crime is between family members. Wife/husband beating, physical or emotional, shootings, kidnappings, and the list goes on. Perhaps if society didn't feel so obligated to their individual bloodline there would be more peace. With the divorce rate around 50%, maybe these people should no longer interact. When folks ask about my brother I have nothing negative to say about him, he is who he is, I just don't feel obligated to struggle with someone simply because my folks had whoopee one night. Family to me doesn't have to be blood: there are stronger ties.

Day Four

ecovery. Ron had to work so I got a chance to sleep in and let my aching muscles regain much needed strength. The afternoon weather was beautiful and it gave me a chance to work on the bike. Changed the oil, tightened things up, made it presentable again. At this point I was about half way through my trip, three quarters of the way through my money, and parts of me felt completely drained. Drug Trip was giving me an extensive education, and my being a slow learner must have compelled Mother Nature to repeat some lessons. If I had known what lay down the road I may well have turned back, but like arriving in Laramie the first time or waking up on the second day of this trip, I anticipated better times. Life is still like that with me. The multiple accidents, head injury, and dark depression that lay ahead would all be fought the same way, it would get better. Not that I wasn't enjoying myself; the trip was grand. The issue I had during the trip was in how evil some people were, for no apparent reason – though is there really ever any reason to be evil?

Going to school in Wyoming meant lots of road trips. It was rare for something significant not to happen. Pharmacy school is normally five years, but as I had serious eye problems one year it took me six years. Over those six years I drove the two thousand and three hundred twenty two miles about sixteen times. That's 37,152 miles of interstate. My first winter there I drove home at Christmas time with my best friend Mark Giard. At the time he owned a red Datsun 240z two-door sports car. We packed the small space with our gear and left Laramie with smiles on our faces and snow in the air. We didn't see black pavement the whole way home. It was not only snowing but tore the myth apart that it gets too cold to snow. Cars littered the highway as they spun out in the winter wonderland. With the CB radio we called in a lot of accidents, but we didn't always stop, like the time in Nebraska when a Chevrolet Corvette zipped past us then promptly spun out. Sorry.

As we approached Chicago the temperature plummeted and the heater in the red car couldn't keep up. As one of us drove, the other slept in a sleeping bag to stay warm. We scraped the frost off the inside of the windows. The fuel line started to freeze. If we kept the speed up around 70mph the engine would keep going, so I did and passed a semi tractor-trailer on a hill and then suddenly lost power. The Z was between two 18-wheelers and the drivers were on the CB talking about us. We'd go fast, have problems, go slow and be between the trucks. Go fast and we would pass them. They thought we were playing with them and they got pissed off. Their plan was to squish us between the two trucks and when the Z was running strong again and I tried to pass, the lead semi would mimic my action, keeping us between the two rigs. Mark got on the CB and explained we were having engine problems. Driver A told us where we could get it fixed and stated he'd also pull over to make sure everything was OK. The truck led the way and pulled into the brightly lit service area and parked out of the way. As soon as I stopped the Z I got out and went over to the truck to personally thank him. When I rapped on the frosty window he jumped up, startled, he had already fallen asleep. The repair was quick and cheap and the driver of the truck A then offered me some amphetamines, which I declined. Mark was asleep when I got lost in New York City and pulled over at a gas station for directions. Somehow the station operator confused me with someone else and thought I was delivering him some drugs. He was adamant that I sell him the non-existent narcotics. Mark woke up and told the guy he was calling the cops if the attendant didn't back off, which he did. Previously I had to tell friends to back off. During one pharmacy class the instructor had shown us the procedure for how a particular drug, a barbiturate, was made. It came out during the question and answer period, that yes, it was fairly easy to do and the process had the nickname of 'Bathtub Barbiturate' as a large batch could be made solely in a bathtub. A 'friend' was pressuring me to make a batch and said if I were a true friend I'd do it for him. When I still declined he offered to pay for my whole five years of college. Until then I had thought of him as a real friend and I told him that if he were a friend he would never ask such a thing of me. He never mentioned it again. OK, time for a lame pharmacy joke… A bear walks into a bar and orders a beer. After a while he gets hungry and eats a patron. The bartender kicks him out. The same thing happens week after week and finally the bartender post a sign; "Bears are NOT allowed to eat the guest". So the bear returns and orders a few beers, then promptly eats a woman. A patron yells, "Hey Bear, can't you read? No eating the guest!" The bear apologizes but the bartender replies, "Oh, that's OK, that was a Bar-Bitch-U-Ate"

The return trip after Christmas proved more eventful, though there was less snow. Accidents were happening all around us. We did well until we hit Nebraska. A short distance before North Platte there was a treacherous patch of black ice. Again, Mark was asleep. About 300 feet in front of me a car had just spun out and ended up in the snowy median. At the time I had the Z at 50mph when whoompf, we started spinning around. While trying to control the car I yelled at Mark who woke up as we were pointed backwards and an 18-wheeler was charging down upon us. He screamed bloody murder and then we hit the shoulder side snow bank sideways and backward, snapping off a mile marker. The car spun one last time then slid down the steep embankment and came to rest buried in snow, literally. The only way out was through the window, which I did while Mark called on the CB for help. As I stepped in front of the car I fell through the snow up to my shoulders. The wheels had passed on either side of a culvert, a foot either way and we would have flipped. After climbing out I first cleared an area around the exhaust pipe so Mark could keep the car running and stay warm, and then I went over to the median and helped push out the other car. The highway was so slick I could slide across both black lanes with one push off from the white snow bank. In the Z Mark told me he got hold of the Nebraska State troopers and help was on the way, and sure enough within minutes a squad car pulled up on the crusty shoulder above us, lights flashing their Christmas colors. Mark went to talk with the Trooper first, as I leaned on the hood on the Z in a field of white. As if in slow motion I saw another car spin out behind the Trooper's. Just like we did, they spun in circles and then, just missing the rear end of the Trooper's car, they hit the snow bank sideways and backwards like we had, and like us they spun one more time. Here I am in a field in Nebraska, off the highway, surrounded by deep snow and a car is coming straight at me! Clambering onto the hood for safety I slipped off the Z as the errant Ford Capri stopped just twenty feet in front of Mark's car. The officer never left his vehicle, but I went over to make sure everyone was fine, and warned them to keep a window cracked open as the four occupants tried to stay warm with the engine running.

When the officer was through with Mark he had me give a statement. At first he just had me sit there and read a morbid article taped to his glove box about what it was like to be a State Trooper and have to pick the spilled brains of an accident victim off the highway. It was complete with bloody details describing various body parts. The Trooper needed a shrink. He accused me of speeding and being reckless, which, for a change, I hadn't been. Then he had me sit with him, wordless, until the tow truck arrived. When the Z hit the tall snow bank the impact blew the driver side tire half way off the alloy rim. We had to empty the contents of the car onto the frozen, windy freeway to get at the spare. Both the weary tow truck operator's and our flashlights were dead. When I asked the morbid Trooper if we could borrow his he refused stating he didn't want to lose it. With a Bic lighter we found the anti-theft lug nut and were able to remove the wheel. The Trooper never got out of his cozy car.

The next winter Mark decided to fly home. Not being able to afford the gas and tolls by myself I went to the campus bulletin board. There I was able to find another student looking to share the driving and gas for the long trip to Maine. Three days prior to Christmas we left Laramie in his yellow Toyota FJ-40. So much for saving gas. We were only halfway through Nebraska when his oddness became apparent. Suddenly he started slapping himself. Hard. He informed me that this was his way of staying alert. When I mentioned that I would be more than happy to take over the driving he declined the offer, and instead pulled into the next Stuckey's to get coffee. The chubby cheerful waitress said it was still brewing but if he gave her the thermos she would fill that instead of using a foam cup. Deal. As we left the building we both paused for no apparent reason. Then, as if on cue, all the snow slid off the roof and landed at our feet, creating a six-foot tall snow bank. Inside the FJ he informed me that in addition to his slapping he would occasionally pour either a hot or cold liquid onto his crotch. Weird. As we were leaving the snowy driveway he asked me to pour him a cup of the fresh brewed coffee. Sure. As I went to hand it to him he hit a chunk of ice and you guessed it, the scalding coffee landed right in his crotch. His yelp was worthy of a horror flick. "Guess you won't have any trouble staying awake", I said as I poured another cup of Joe.

The heater in the Toyota didn't work well. All through the trip we would have to scrape the inside of the windows, and it wasn't even as cold out as the year before. By the time we reached the east coast we were both spent. His idea was to visit a commune in Connecticut that he had lived in years ago. It would take us hours from our route and I asked that we just dive the final five hours and go home. Not being a democracy I was ignored and we headed off to what he called the first modern commune in America. We arrived late at night and he was all excited. Being a gentleman he offered me the mattress. At first I was ready to accept the offer, then I noticed that the sheet covering the well-worn pad wasn't intended to be dark gray, if you looked closely at the corners you could tell it had once been a white sheet. Being as polite as possible I told him I actually preferred my sleeping bag and I headed back out into the cold to fetch it. Morning, that time of fresh starts and endless possibilities came all too soon. Being a sound sleeper it must have taken the fair maiden several nudges to awaken me. Lying on my back I opened my eyes, and oh, what a sight to behold. She was standing above me with a leg on either side of my head. Her short, used to be white nightie, barely reached her waist. She must have been playing with herself as she nudged me awake, for there in all its glory was her womanhood fully exposed to me. "Hi". "Hello". "Want anything to eat?" "No thanks, I'm fine". Unperturbed she went off in search of someone more fulfilling. Breakfast was ready and my co-driver called me downstairs. The house members had formed a circle in the cool kitchen then one of them grabbed a fresh box of cereal and poured the entire contents into the chipped bowl, then promptly added a quart of whole milk. The chef ate for a few minutes then passed the bowl to the next person, and so on. When my time arrived I declined and stated I preferred fruit (not the type I was surrounded by) and went to the FJ to retrieve my frozen orange.

The summer previous to the drug trip I worked in Wyoming. In mid August I took two weeks off so I could go home. It took me just over forty hours to travel the 2,300 miles, alone. In Iowa I was with a convoy of about twenty vehicles, mostly eighteen-wheelers, and we were doing 100mph plus, instead of the usual 80 to 90mph. It was nighttime and we must have felt invisible. At one point I decided to go from the rear of the group to the lead and I buried the needle at over 120mph. For some reason the topic of tires came up on the CB radio and someone asked me what I was running, as radials were still fairly new. When I mentioned I was running retreads, bias ply tires that were used and then a new outer shell vulcanized on, I caught a lot of flak from the concerned truck drivers. "Are you nuts?" When I asked why I was told retreads can't handle high speed and I was strongly advised to slow down. Just as I hit 65mph the right rear tire blew apart, never to be seen again. Itsy bitsy pieces. My days at Vedauwoo proved useful and I was able to control the Chrysler without incident.

In no time flat I was back on the road. The next afternoon when I was in Illinois a big black Cadillac was on the shoulder with a deflated tire. With my car parked like a police officer's, so I had protection from oncoming traffic, I went to the driver's window and asked if she needed help. The female driver was huge; I'm talking 300 plus pounds. Obviously she couldn't change the tire, and since she didn't have a CB radio to call for help, I offered to. Only problem was her jack was missing and mine was buried under fifteen cases of Coors.

At that time Coors wasn't sold east of the Mississippi. So there I was, nineteen years old, with fifteen cases of beer stacked next to my car as I changed her flat.

Thankfully no state troopers came into sight. She was very gracious and insisted I take the twenty dollars, so, to be polite, I did. Being flush with cash I pulled into the next town and went to McDonald's. The neighborhood I drove through was incredible: brick sidewalks, brick crossways, brick homes, overhanging trees, yet something felt plastic. Maybe it's an Illinois thing, but here at the Mc-E-D's was an identical black car with another huge woman driver. When she got out of her Cadillac you could almost hear the car sigh. She first attempted to go straight through the main door of the shiny new building, but she was too wide. She then turned sideways and tried to squish through. Temporarily stuck halfway, with one breast in and one breast out, she was unfazed and managed to free herself from the opening by wiggling back and forth. Not one to let a fry run loose, she got in her car, which gave another sigh, and went to the drive up window.

After a two-hour nap at a rest stop with 'No Napping' signs, I got back on the boring interstate. The remainder of the ride was tough, Coke wasn't strong enough and Jolt hadn't been introduced yet. The miles just dragged by, painfully slow. Everything blended together, reflexes were on autopilot, and to be honest, I couldn't remember what town, or at times, what state I was in. At Boston I almost pulled over to sleep and it is only through sheer luck that I didn't have an accident. The desire to get home, be with family and friends, over-rode common sense and I pushed on till I reached the familiar front door. My parents were just heading out to eat, an uncommon event for them, when I showed up at home around 6:00PM. After quick hugs, kisses and handshakes I told them I was going to nap and see them when they got back from dinner. My Dad was amazed that I had traveled so far so quickly. The sun was bright when pounding on the door awakened me. It was my parents. Did I fall asleep that quickly? Did they forget something? My mom started laughing and I couldn't figure out what was wrong. Not only was it morning, it was forty hours later. They had locked themselves out, as they were sure a full days sleep would be sufficient for me and so I would be up when they returned. I had slept through a whole day and a half. It was the last time I drove straight through, as in the end it was no quicker and certainly no safer.

Day Five

on's female roommate made an incredible amount of noise that morning. Slamming doors, banging pots and stomping her feet. Lying on the couch, I ignored it all, pretended to sleep and waited for Ron to get up. We agreed to meet for breakfast but it took me much longer to pack the bike and find my way on the Yamaha then it did for him to jump on his Raleigh bicycle and get there. Consequently we didn't have much time for each other and it would be almost ten years before we would see each other again, in North Conway, NH, which is where I continued my 'close call' adventures.

Before Santa Barbara, I had seen Ron one previous time since I left for Wyoming. He had sold his bike shop and moved to England for a while to study bicycles with his mentor. After his stint in England he drove across the U.S. with a mutual friend who's name is now lost in my gray matter. One winter night, without forewarning, I answered my door, which to confuse others I had mounted two sets of hinges on so that the door swung out instead of in. There were also two doorknobs. First visitors would get the wrong doorknob, then they would push in; frustrated, they would grab the other knob, yet still push in. Cheap amusement. At the Kappa Sigma fraternity,

Ron had simply found the right door, pounded, and yelled "Lawyer".

Being PV (pre vegan), we were able to have our standard pepperoni pizza and beer. He had loved London and talked incessantly about punk rock, surely a quick fad. His days of Jackson Brown were left back in Maine. The following morning classes demanded my attention and the road west beckoned to him. Thirty years later he still loves California though how he lives without a Maine winter is beyond me. Ayuh.

By my junior year I was living with Ray in the large basement apartment. We were 'off-campus' brothers of the fraternity. One night the social director failed to inform Ray and myself of a function. Big mistake. We took the opportunity to rig the house while everyone else was in a secret basement room. First the bedroom door hinges, we removed the pins. Secondly, we greased the underside of the doorknobs. On to the bathrooms, where we used gelatin to set up two of the toilet bowls, while on the other bowls we stretched saran wrap. Knowing how to wire the phone switchboard allowed me to send calls to the wrong rooms. We also put sardine juice behind some radiators. OK, that was cruel. Less cruel was to loosen the light bulbs then turn off the circuit breakers. Next function we were invited just so they could keep an eye on us.

Campus life agreed with me, and probably most others. When I had arrived in Laramie the first person I spoke with was at the desk of the thirteen-story dorm I was assigned to. He asked me if a room on the eight floor would be OK. "Sure" Except I pronounced it like a true Mainer and it came out more like Sho-ah. "Your from Boston, aren't you?" Well, to a Maniac that was an insult, but I said I understood his western drawl just fine and knew what he meant. He stated he didn't have an accent and I replied that back home neither did I. Thinking I was in fine shape I took my first load up using the stairs. Damn! It was explained to me that it would take several days to adjust to the altitude and even more for the attitude! Living with a complete stranger was an eye-opener. While we got along fine, we certainly would never become best friends. He was from PA and considered that the center of the universe. Of the two guys next door, one was more like me and the other like my roommate, my roommate and his twin would use the room next door to partake in the wacky tobacky, while the other guy and myself were at the library. After climbing the eight flights of stairs one night I could smell that smell and knew what they were up to. Without giving it a second thought I pounded loudly on their door and shouted "Open up, it's the Police", then I went to my room figuring they would recognize my voice and find it funny. Wrong. As I got ready for bed I heard the window next door open and heard a lot of commotion. About a half hour later, as I was dozing off to sleep, my roommate returned all shaken up. "Man, you wouldn't believe what happened to us. Cops pounded on our door but we acted like we weren't there and they went away. Just in case they busted in we played it safe and threw our stash out the window" On another evening Mr. Wacky Tabacky and I were shooting the breeze and for whatever reason he asked me what type of furnace we used back home. In a previous conversation he had already alluded to the fact that he considered Maine to be extremely backward and out of date. One of his very first questions had been if there are a lot of bears in the city; "Only a few, we keep dogs to scare them off" Not having a real clue as to the type of furnace in our home, I said 'central'. "Isn't that a pain in the ass?" "No, only when it's your turn" "What do you mean, 'your turn'?" "Well, as you know, our town has one central furnace and one week a month it's my sister and my duties to keep it stoked. We have to get up early in the morning and fill it up with wood and coal and then make sure all the pipes that run to the other homes are in good shape" He look dumbfounded and his lower jaw was actually dropped. Finally I couldn't help myself and started laughing. Later in the semester I was talking to a friend from Illinois (whatever you do, don't say IllinOISE) and told him of the furnace story. He too had a backward view of Maine, but he said he wouldn't have fallen for the story. At that I felt challenged so I said it was almost to bad I made the furnace story up for now I doubt I could get him to believe what we do with our potato skins. That was the bait and he ate it. "Well, as you're probably aware, Maine is a poor state with limited resources. While the state is large geographically, it has a small population, so paying for roads is a major problem. A couple years ago we ran an experiment and found out if we recycle our potato skins and add them to the asphalt when it is being mixed, not only does the tar last longer, it saves us a bundle of money. The State started a potato skin collection initiative and now everyone puts their potato skins out with their trash so the skins will keep our taxes down". "Wow, and the roads hold up?" Again I couldn't take it and busted a gut.

It was fairly cool that morning as I headed south toward the smog filled booming metropolis called Los Angeles. Nothing there demanded my attention and I was looking forward to driving in the desert, so I banked a left. The drive over the mountains was breathtaking, and the drive down the mountains was exhilarating. While it was late autumn there was still plenty of color and traffic was sparse. Almost Zen again. My poor abused Yamaha was now leaking a fair amount of fork fluid and I would have to break down and find a mechanic. Barstow was only a couple hundred miles away and I planned to make it there by noon. The dry heat of desert felt great as I pulled into a motorcycle shop. As soon as I pulled in an employee greeted me. So hospitable. After explaining my situation he told me there was a yummy lunch counter with home made pie directly across the street. He said that by the time I got back the bike would be ready and I could continue my trip.

Small diners offer some of the best meals I've ever had. While they tend not to be fancy there is something to be said about the honesty of the owner run diner. The motorcycle shop employee had been dead on; this was a great place. As I was in no rush, pie it was. Chocolate banana cream, and to make doubly sure, slide a piece of that apple pie over as well. Yeah, great pie. After finishing my second Coke I ambled back over to the bike shop. The beat up Yamaha was right where I had left it; only something was different. It was obvious the forks hadn't been touched, I could still see oil dripping down, but the backpack was open. The borrowed orange hi-tech tent, down mittens and some other gear was missing. I was robbed. When I approached the friendly employee who had sent me to the yummy diner he asked what I wanted. "I'd like to call the police, I've been robbed". As I described what was missing we walked toward the bike. Things got weird. He denied ever having seen me before and didn't know why the bike was there and he wanted to look through the backpack. When I found John's new Cannon 35mm camera and extra lens, buried deep in the pack, I sighed and he exclaimed; "well you still have the camera!". Several times he repeated this. Then he finished off with; "What are you complaining about, you STILL have the CAMERA" He couldn't take his eyes off the camera. When another employee got involved it became obvious this was no battle I was going to win. They knew the sheriff by name. Me? Some dusty beat-up kid from Wyoming, slandering the fine name of these honest, hard-working employees. At least lunch was tasty. The shop stank.

Thoughts raced through my mind as I headed out of town. Return at night and smash the windows, no, burn it down! Yeah, then I could rot in some podunk desert town with no chance at redemption.

Better to keep on moving. The forks were so bad that every time I used the front brake the front end of the bike would nosedive and it would be hard to control. Such mixed feelings. Never had I been set up like that before. There was anger both at the thief and myself. More than once I had been robbed, but this was different.

When I was younger Ron and I were walking on Forest Ave, a busy road, around noontime on a Saturday when two thugs approached us and wanted our money. Thug 1 looked vaguely familiar to me, and he must have sensed it for just as quickly as the assault started he pulled his friend off of me and ran down the street. Another time, when I was a freshman in high school I had a job at the Portlander, a motel/restaurant on Congress St, downtown Portland, a several mile walk for me. My job was being the lone busboy for six bustling waitresses. They would load the trays as high as possible and I was required by management to balance the tray on one hand and carry it over patron's heads. The only spill I ever had was just as I was lowering onto the counter in the kitchen. The crusty old cigarette-smoking dishwasher had befriended me, and he told me he would tell management the $8.00 blue goblin was already cracked. He and I shared secrets, which in today's world would shock people: uneaten buns, French fries, even steak, were recycled – maybe they were just ahead of their time! My pay was $1.00 per hour plus part of the tips. With the money wadded up in my front pocket I was walking down Forest Ave at about 10:00PM(yes, same street!) when three punks ran across the street and pinned me to the AT&T building. After I was punched and choked, my hands pinned behind my back, one of the assaulters who had put his hand in my money laden pocket exclaimed that I had nothing and the three of them threw me to the ground and ran off. Back in California, Zen was gone.

Again this trip was showing me both the good and bad of earth's occupants. Why must people be so greedy, deceitful, and violent? It can't all be blamed on how one was raised; there must be some basic difference in how a brain is wired. What makes one person left hand-ed or right handed, tall or short, straight or gay? Answers must lie in our basic chemistry; while our DNA is 99.6% similar to monkeys, most people wouldn't want to date one, so perhaps this disposition to be mean is unavoidable in some people. When I was young my folks would take us to church each week, partly in an attempt to teach us to behave in a moral and just way. If anyone understood good and evil, my folks did, for WWII had showed them the true potential of humans. Both had witnessed things they would only rarely talk about, and when they did their demeanor would always change. No movie could ever frighten them, for they had been at the brink of humanity. I loved my folks. Saint Joseph's is a beautiful stone-faced, stained glass, gothic church. One of everyone's favorite priests there was the fire and brimstone lecturer Father Luzon. No one slept through a Luzon mass. He didn't use the microphone like other priest, his booming voice would echo of the cold stonewalls and make your blood boil. Outside of the church he was quieter, but still held a large presence. I, like other kids, was in awe of him. Next to the church, and sharing the same driveway, is a Catholic school run by the church. School was exactly one mile from our home and the Hurtubise kids would trod though sun, rain, sleet and snow to attend school, which was rarely canceled. Dana, Monica and I would make the journey many times. Starting in first grade I would have breakfast with my siblings then grab my lunch for the day and head out the door. Several times every year, especially the early grade years, I would forget my sack lunch on the counter. Mom didn't drive and we still had 'party lines' on our phones; cell phones were only seen in the comic strips on Dick Tracy's wrist, and a party line meant you couldn't afford a dedicated line; if you picked up the heavy black receiver you may well be interrupting someone else's conversation. When lunchtime would arrive I would sit quietly at my desk, hoping the nun in charge didn't notice. More often than not my 'lack-o-lunch' would be observed by the eagle-eyed penguin. My sorry butt would be dragged to the white convent, also in the same parking lot, and I would be spanked and told what a poor mother I must have; letting her child leave without his lunch. After the spanking I would be given a peanut butter and jelly sandwich along with a glass of cold milk. Arriving home I wouldn't tell my folks about the spanking, as I had been told not to by the religious, closer to god, nuns, rather I would simply let mom know that the feel good nuns had provided me with a lunch. Mom not only took care of the four of us but also worked about thirty hours a week at the local A&P Supermarket, to which she also walked.

When I was in third grade I slipped at the top of the stairs in our home. Why do old homes have 13 steps? To get from one floor to another. A large nail with an oversized head was sticking out of the carpet, and when my right knee made contact the nail won. Standing up I noticed something felt funny against my leg, so I went into the bathroom to have a look. A thick chunk of meat was hanging on by a thin slice of skin. With my hand holding it in place I went to see my dad, who was sitting in his favorite black leather chair while he smoked a pipe. "Dad, I need to go the hospital". "Oh, why?" With my hand removed the chunk of meat fell against my leg. "Lets' go". At the hospital he held my hand and told me how brave I was while the young doctor attended to my knee. Thirteen stitches and a tightly wound bandage later and we were back home. Getting to school proved a bit more difficult as I was not to bend my knee for two weeks. During the fire drill the next day at school we were told that if we were injured we should use the left side of the stairs and stand outside in a separate group, while the remaining kids used the right side of the stairs. As going up and down stairs was difficult, I followed my friend who was using crutches. He was faster. A religious compassionate thoughtful nun walked up to us, and without so much as a word grabbed me by the collar and literally threw me into the other group. All thirteen stitches were ripped out. As my crying wouldn't stop, the nuns eventually sent me home after lunch. The mile walk with ripped stitches was grueling. When I got home I told my mom what had happened and she managed to reach my dad. When we returned from round two at the hospital, my Dad called the convent: seldom have I heard him scream while on a telephone, but he was in rare form that day. The nuns apologized profusely to my parents, but never said a word to me and didn't so much as acknowledge that I had a physical problem. Later, when I was in sixth grade, I met up with more of the Catholic Church's godliness. It was sunny and warm and we had just been released into the paved back play yard for lunch recess when father Luzon approached me. He asked if I could help him move some boxes in the church basement, where he collected clothes for the needy. "Sure". He led the decent along the steep dark stairs and into the dimly lit room, chock full of cardboard boxes. His hand was always on my shoulder, guiding me through his sanctuary. It would take place several times like this over the course of the year. Every time he would give me the stern warning not to tell my parents, or else damnation would befall us all. Scared beyond belief, shivering and thinking of somewhere else, I would do as I was told time and again. If there is a hell, it should be home for the child abusers of the world. Later the church, after many complaints, would move father Luzon to South America; where innocent children and not the long arm of the law would surround him. Decades later I would see father Luzon one last time. All dressed in his flowing expensive garments, the brilliant white robe and yellow, red and green accessories, as a ghost, as I exited the shower in my bathroom, he looked unapologetic right into my eyes, as real and solid as any person can look, on the day that he died, and hours before I heard the news.

The feeling of abuse from the mechanic made me reflect on other times I was abused. It would be miles before my blood ceased to boil over. Friends had trusted me with their possessions and I felt I had betrayed them. When I got back to Wyoming Ray said to forget about the mittens, but I got him a new pair. Wayne definitely wanted the tent replaced. At the time it was high tech and cost over three hundred dollars. More than I had spent for the bike. Wayne came from money, but that didn't lessen my obligation. A friend of Wayne's worked for a local sporting goods store and said he'd give me his substantial discount. Two hundred dollars! Took me months to earn the money. Only later would I learn that the friend's discount was the five-finger kind and he and Wayne used the money for drugs. Drug Trip. At one point, years later, Wayne would tell me how envious he was of me. He said everything was given to him; he didn't have to work after school or on weekends to raise money not just for toys but to be able to eat. He made it sound romantic that I had to scrape by most of the time. He must have been on drugs. For some reason he wouldn't trade places... that's just for TV.

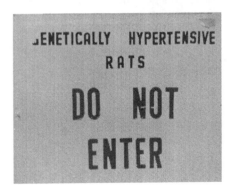

The previous winter, I had not only had my work-study job, but I washed UPS trucks three days a week; twice during the weekdays and also on Saturday. This was in addition to my rat-feeding job.

UPS was strict. No shortcuts. So I would be alone washing these big trucks and the phone would ring. Often it would be a UPS driver asking me to disconnect his radio and hide it, as a radio was punishable by termination. Other times it would be the garage owner calling to ask if any UPS drivers had radios. Never saw one. During the winter break all my fraternity brothers were gone, off to their warm homes or ski lodges. The work-study program paid biweekly, as did the UPS job. At the start of the week vacation I was out of cash and my Dad's business was going through a slow period and the price of home heating oil had skyrocketed. They were having such a tough time my Dad hung an electric blanket in front of the entryway in hopes of decreasing rising fuel cost. My folks had also installed an incredibly ugly tan woodstove in our beautiful living room that was decorated with mom's hand sewn velvet dark green curtains. They burned several cords of hardwood each winter, which my brothers and I split during the summer. There was no way I could call and ask them for money. With no one around the large fraternity house I filled my days doing homework, house chores, and taking hikes in Vedauwoo. No money for food but I had five pounds of popcorn, a popper, some oil, and 'butter salt', "If it doesn't taste like real butter we'll give you your money back!" 'Include $4.99 for handling cost'. Yum. For five days all I ate was chemically altered popcorn. On the final Friday night and early Saturday morning, when friends were starting to return, we had a huge blizzard. High winds are not uncommon in Wyoming, but this was a record setter. When I went to wash the UPS trucks the snowdrift was literally as tall as the one story garage. Washing the trucks required me to shuffle them around, and I would normally park one on the street as I washed the others. There was little extra room in that garage; the overhead doors were only slightly wider than the trucks and the large chrome truck mirrors would have to be folded in to get the trucks in or out of the garage. With the rear garage overhead door open all I could see was

87

a wall of white. A call to the Denver office was fruitless. A snowdrift to them was something you stumbled over. "Just drive through it". Some part of the brain of the UPS man in Denver wasn't functioning correctly. "It's as tall as the building". "Just drive through it". Then the Denver man was upset when I called later and told him we needed a wrecker to get the truck unstuck.

A hundred miles and Barstow was melting from my mind, though never forgotten. Desert driving is bliss. Wide open scenery, warm weather, and seldom any traffic. The Mohave Desert proved a challenge for the battered Yamaha, as it didn't care for the heat. When I first moved to Wyoming I didn't care for the desert, that was before I got to know it. On the CB radio I would call out "breaker breaker for a tree". After spending six years in Wyoming and returning to Maine, all the trees made me feel claustrophobic. Gas mileage was poor since I was driving the bike to its limit. The spare gallon of gas came in handy yet again, though this time it was only three-quarters full. The multiple falls and crashes had created a pinhole in the seam of the cheap red and yellow metal can. Nothing quite like watching gas sizzle on a scorching hot exhaust pipe, at least I wasn't pinned under it this time. The extra fuel was enough to get me to the next station and toward my day's destination, Flagstaff, Arizona. There was a chapter of the Kappa Sigma fraternity there and that meant a safe place to stay, as now I was tent less, and a hot shower was calling my name.

The warm day gave way to a cool night. It was great driving weather, especially for the end of October. Just a few miles outside of the city limits I started to hear some weird noises. The highway was almost deserted so I knew it wasn't from another vehicle. It was an odd screeching sound, perfectly at home in an Alfred Hitchcock movie. Slowing the bike down did not get rid of it, so I sped back up. As there was no other traffic, I turned on my high beams. Birds! Massive, low flying birds! Felt like winged pterodactyls were above me. While doing 70mph I could see one of the kamikaze attackers at head level. He, (she?), wasn't backing off. Playing chicken with a chicken relative. Literally ducking to avoid being hit, the huge bird swept right over my right shoulder, talons brushing past my helmet. It's tough changing your shorts on the road.

It was easy to find the frat house, and this was before GPS! Being Halloween night, a costume party was in full swing. Some of the out-fits were really well done. The most impressive to me was a guy dressed as The Incredible Hulk. Obviously he was a body builder as he was ripped with massive arms and washboard abs, his shirt and shorts were also ripped with his bulging muscles protruding out. The shorts were short and tight and left little to the imagination, unlike the T.V. series. His skin had just the right tone of green, befitting the popular Hulk character. He enjoyed being watched by any and everyone. Other than on television, I had never seen anyone like him. My attention to him was picked up bye others. When things finally wound down and it was time to crash I found a spot at the top of the stairs to unroll my battered sleeping bag. A guy in the room nearest to me invited me to share his room, as people would probably trip over me in the middle of the night. After moving my gear into his room he mentioned there was plenty of room in his bed, it stayed that way. The floor was good.

Knowing alcohol well, I had fit right into that event. It was a nice time, as there were no mean drunks, no fighting, just a silly Halloween party. There had been times in Laramie that after drink-ing I would run into people, literally. Seems I'm one of those stupid drunks. No meanness or name calling, just stupid acts by yours truly. Stairs would pose a special problem for me when I had a few too many. 'The Buck', a popular watering hole in Laramie, was a two-floor bar. Uh Oh. Any night was fun there, but like most bars, Friday and Saturday nights were the liveliest. After watching yet another wet T-shirt contest, that one that had Mark's current girlfriend as one of the most popular, though not biggest, girls, I found myself having problems with my torso. It seemed the floor was calling. My friend suggested it was time to go home and I was fine with that. Just those damn stairs. As I rounded the corner at the top of the tall long steep flight of stairs I noticed that there was still a line of people waiting to get in. Having taken bowling as my elective to fulfill my Phys. Ed. requirement prepared me, if not the unknowing pins down below. After the first step I was tucked in and speeding toward a strike. The bouncer noticed the human bowling ball but it was too late. "Looook ooooooooout!!" A split wasn't bad, as the folks on the edges managed to escape, but mayhem ruled the night and a huge pile of bodies littered the entryway as I continued my way out the door and to the street's gutter.

After that night it became common knowledge at the frat house that if I had a few too many, clear the stairs. Of course being college students some found this to be a source of amusement. Amazingly I was never hurt, though several bottles of Mickey's wide mouth ale met an untimely demise. My frat brothers also found out I got extremely ticklish when drunk. Then the two were combined so from the third floor to the basement I would be tickled and rolled down the stairs to where I would fall asleep. Seems I sleep rather soundly when drunk for I would wake up in the strangest places. Wrong room. Bushes outside. Telephone booth.

When I was a freshman a fellow pledge and I tried to drain the keg. By the way, what do Coors Light and having sex in a canoe have in common? They are both close to water. Anyway, after we were both stuttering drunk, someone mentioned we should go sing our pledge song to all the sororities. The sororities were all lined up across the field. Pretty pink houses, OK, brick and whatever. At the first house the girls were nice and cheered us on. Our singing wasn't half bad, all things considered. At the last house the front lights were turned on and we could hear commotion from inside. The front door exploded open and out rushed a dozen football players. Evidently we had sung our serenade to the University's football dorm house. They chased us across the way and let us go without pummeling us into the ground.

Drinking off private property was strictly forbidden and campus police would often be near a frat party waiting for the unfortunate misstep. This, to me, was a challenge. The distance from fraternity row across a one-lane road, then over the field and across another one lane road to sorority row is probably only a couple hundred feet. The edges of the field have tall, mature pine trees. One particular night the campus police were out in full force. There must have been twenty police monitoring a small fraternity/sorority party. My girlfriend had left early to study, silly girl. Now my immature buddies and I were talking about the absurdity of it all when an idea stuck me. With a clean, fresh plastic Coors cup I went into the frat house and got some water. My buddies and I were talking when I told them I was going to go check on my girlfriend. They weren't aware I was drinking water so they proclaimed loudly for me to leave my cup behind. Ears of the campus police were burning. With no further warning I bolted off toward Sorority Row. The police were taken aback. Screaming for me to stop I could hear one shout, "Get him". Being young has its advantages and I was able to run through the trees on the far side before the campus police could catch me. With heart pounding and lungs scorched I pounded on the back door of the sorority. My girlfriend said I was nuts and as she needed to study I should return to the party. So I did. Out the front door with Coors cup in hand I sprinted back toward the fraternity. Four campus officers leaped out from behind a pine tree and captured me. "Why are you running?" "Exercise". "Why didn't you stop before?" "Didn't think you were talking to me". "What's in the cup?" "Water". "Water?" "Water". The Coors cup was passed from officer to officer. The water was cold but they were steaming. Finally one officer takes a sip. "Water". It was the last time we saw such a show of force by the campus police for a small party. In the future it would be State Police protecting me instead of Campus Police chasing me.

Yeah, that's me, before I could save up and buy the sleeves. I'm standing at the beginning of Fraternity Row. In the background you can see what I once thought was the last sorority house but was actually the football team's house. The pine trees in the middle are where the campus police were hiding waiting for my return to Fraternity Row (and the infamous cup of water).

Day Six

The frat house in Flagstaff was a disaster. Not Animal House bad, but a mess. After pitching in with the cleaning for a bit, I went and packed my bike. It was cool outside but I felt refreshed. With an extra layer on I started up the Yamaha and headed off toward Albuquerque New Mexico. It would be another long day on the bike but I looked forward to the desert drive. No screeching birds, no employees setting me up, just a nice quiet day. Arizona has stunning scenery and a great climate. Might end up there some day.

Never am I bored while driving a motorcycle, it may be due to how it's different to the senses than driving in a car, even a convertible. When on a bike I feel more connected to the road. Without a roof or thick pillars I tend to notice more things (except the occasional hairpin warning sign!). Olfactory senses seem heightened; did that cow fart? The actual road surface feel is transmitted through the handlebars, whoa, pebbles. Driving a bike just made me more alert, to bad the alertness died when I turned the key off. My freshman year of college I took a 'get-fit' P.E. class and learned how out of shape I was. The whole class made great strides (again, no pun intended), running better than ever and doing an intensive workout with no weight sets. At the end of one session I was all pumped up and was changing into my street clothes when a couple of young teenagers came into the locker-room. One of them asked me if I was strong enough to pick him up and I said I was, of course he wanted proof. While I had been in that lock-room a bunch of times, I never really looked at the ceiling, which was, after all, a pretty standard ceiling. When I grabbed him on either side of the waist I lifted him quickly and let him go, intending to catch him on the rebound. What I didn't anticipate was his head going completely through the white ceiling. Amidst a cloud of sheetrock dust and chunks I grabbed him, set him down and asked if he was OK. OK? He was thrilled! "Do it again. Do it again." "My turn, my turn" yelled his buddy. At that point I made a hasty exit and avoided the locker-room for some time.

Leaving Flagstaff I thought I would tire out quickly, but I proved myself wrong. I could ride all day. Six, seven, I've done eight hundred miles on a bike in one day. On one trip I logged five hundred fifty miles, the whole time with intense rain and wind, on Interstate 80 at highway speeds. It used to be a wonderful escape for me, one I hope to return to someday. An auto accident knocked me out of commission for eight years, but that's another story! Back then I could ride forever. Its weird, but I wouldn't even remember stopping for gas. Ask me about a landmark and I could tell you the weather conditions for that day, how the landmark looked, how I felt…

Previous to getting the Yamaha in Laramie all I had owned was a Benelli 175cc mini bike. It was a big engine on a small bike and tiny wheels. Everyone called me the mosquito because of the noise the bike made though few could keep up with me. At the time I was a freshman in high school and my Dad, who tried selling Benelli Motorcycles at his gas station, promised me the bike if I got a scholarship into Cheverus, the preparatory high school my oldest brother had gone to. While I only got a half scholarship, he kept up his end of the deal. By using railroad ways and trails I was able to go all around the city. Literally. By sophomore year the bike was gone; Dad needed the money to help heat our home, but the driving skills I learned stayed with me.

In order to pay the other half of school tuition my folks said I would need to pay for half of their amount. So I got a newspaper route with the Portland Evening Express, now defunct. It was an easy way to come up with my share. Having the evening route (there was also a morning route) meant I had to take the Sunday morning route also. Usually not a problem for me, until that first Christmas. On Christmas Eve Monica, Leo, and myself were all in the kitchen with Monica baking cookies and I supervising. Leo decided it would be fun to pour a full bottle of molasses over my head. Angry, I ran up to his room, dripping goo along the way. Screaming that I was going to knock his precious stereo over I stomped my feet on the maple floor, directly above the kitchen. After gaining control of my senses, I left well enough alone and proceeded to go downstairs. Leo had rushed by me to check on his cherished Harmon Kardon. Part way down our stairs a hallway passed over the stairs; I was in the habit of jumping up, grabbing a couple of rails and swinging back and forth over the steps. As I was doing this Leo came down the steps behind me. He had no reason to be angry because I didn't touch anything in his sanctuary, yet for what ever reason, as I was swinging forward Leo took the opportunity to harass me again. This time he placed his foot on my butt and pushed me off the rail as I was swinging forward. Free flight is a magical thing. Landing sucks. The large wooden ball on the last banister made a heavy impact on my chest. After that I flipped over and smashed into the tall iron radiator in the narrow hallway. Momentarily I lost consciousness. When I came to I remember Leo hovering over me while Monica was nonchalantly walking past the far end of the hallway. She paused, looked at Leo and said; "Well, you've always wanted to kill him and now you've done it".

Leo was mortified at his actions. He quickly scooped me up and put me in his Ford Capri, which had chains on the tires. The iron radiator must have made good contact with my head, for I don't remember anything until I woke up in the E.R. It was the same E.R. the police officer had taken me to years before. The pavement in our driveway retained the scooped out areas of Leo's actions for years to come, as his chains dug divots into the frozen blacktop. After getting to the hospital I waited hours before being seen. Maybe it was the molasses. On the night of Christmas Eve I was discharged with a cracked rib. No Oxycontin back then, just 'take two aspirin and buck up'. On Christmas morning I had to deliver newspapers, pulling my red wagon with its wood slat side rails through the fresh snow. Near my last stop I had to go down an alleyway that had always creeped me out. Dark and narrow, certainly not a place you'd want to go to after seeing To Kill a Mockingbird. Just as I was passing a large banged up dumpster a monstrous black cat screeched and leapt out of the container and landed at my feet. Not a soul was resting. The scream heard round the city. When I told Ron he thought it was hilarious; so much so he said it CRACKED him up, much like my rib. He'd try to get me laughing about it, but it hurt too much to laugh, so I punched him.

The winter before my drug trip I had brought a load of fireworks back with me. In Wyoming fireworks were often sold at roadside stands, kinda like vegetable stands back home, only different. In Laramie we would set a whole gross of bottle rockets in a can, aim them at sorority row and light them off. Cheap thrills. In Maine you couldn't get bottle rockets. What better way to help finance my studies than to bring back some pyrotechnics? Monica had moved into the same building that Leo and his first wife occupied years earlier. It was near the University of Southern Maine, on a narrow snow choked pothole riddled street. My brother Dana gave me a ride. We had to park his large car on another street as Fesseden Street was packed. To announce our arrival Dana and I thought we should shoot some bottle rockets at Monica's apartment. Only problem was they went too far and blew up down the street. When we asked Monica if she heard them she said no and doubted anyone would since everyone had his or her windows shut. Shortly after settling in at the Christmas Eve party I noticed a lot of police cars going down the street. Dana and I were curious so we decided to go outside and investigate. As soon as we left the building a police officer shouted at us to drop to the ground. Cops were everywhere, pistols drawn, special response units, just like at the California motel. Prone and shaken, we asked what was going on. Apparently several gunshots had been fired at a lawyer's house down the street. The officer asked if we had heard anything. "No, all the windows are shut, we didn't hear a thing"

Bottle rockets could liven up most any event. During the summer of 1976 Mark had bought a red Triumph TR6, a fantastic looking car, but you had better have deep pockets to own one. When Mark showed up with his new used car I asked how the brakes and electrical systems were, after all it was a British Leyland product. Mark was an eternal optimist, "great". On the way to Boston for the bicentennial celebrations the left front brake pad disintegrated with a howl straight from hell. We kept going. Later in the day we were following our friends in some slow moving traffic when yet another opportunity to fire bottle rockets presented itself. We did learn, though, that at about 30mph the wind force against the rocket is stronger than the rocket. So when I held the bottle rocket out the window and tried to fire upon our friends in a car ahead, the rocket stayed in place and blew up beside me. Mark thought that was funnier than if it had worked. When traffic came to another crawl I tried again. Beautiful. We could hear the 'whoosh' as the rocket flew past our friend's car and went straight up the row of vehicles. It blew up right in front of a police officer. He had to change his pants so we were never caught. After drinking... er celebrating, the bicentennial, we all gathered at an all-night restaurant. The meal was going grand when police showed up. Being paranoid we thought they had figured out the bottle rocket incident. Then several fire trucks showed up. Firemen ran toward the restaurant. Hmmm. Ladders were being slapped up against the two-story building; hoses were dragged across the lawn, men in uniforms running about and general commotion. It happened all in a matter of minutes. The second story was on fire and the waitress was still serving us breakfast with a smile.

At the frat house I had felt genuinely welcome. That was an uncommon experience for me, as I am basically a loner. At most, all I ever have is a couple close friends. To most people I come across as cold. This may be the result of my analytical way of thinking. When I comment on how something is done I don't mean to sound superior, I'm just curious why it was done the way it was. Most people know better than to ask me for my opinion as I seldom sugar coat it. When I was in therapy for my traumatic brain injury (is there a NON-traumatic brain injury?) my shrink at the time told me that he could envision me living in a log cabin in Wyoming, alone and happy. That is probably true, head injury or no head injury. There are times I like being the class clown but I also value my alone time. Fitting in seamlessly at the frat house was uncommon. Maybe it was the beer, or being on my drug trip, or those funny tasting brownies they gave me. Kidding. During the second semester we had to eat at the dorm's cafeteria, as the frat house suffered major damage due to a broken water pipe. It was a nice change of pace for me, as I didn't have to clean up after forty guys but of course that meant I needed a new job. The trudge over to the cafeteria was filled with snowball fights and general hijinks. To break things up even further, one day a few of us thought we would go with fake broken limbs, so the pretty girls behind the counter would serve us. By the time we entered the building everyone but me had backed out, and I wasn't faking a broken arm. My legs are more flexible than most, so I loosened my belt, bent my leg backwards, and stuck my foot up through my belt and wore an overcoat. As I entered the line every thing was going according to plan and a gorgeous young lady grabbed a tray and helped me out, asking what I'd like for dinner and would I like dessert. As we approached a table full of students it would get very quiet, for an amputee was approaching and god knows you can't laugh when someone seriously hurt is near you. When we passed that same table enormous laughter would erupt, and this quiet/loud effect continued until my innocent helper found me a table toward the center of the cavernous room. First she set my tray down then helped me with my crutches. As I sat down I undid the belt buckle and let my leg slip back to its normal position without her noticing. Ever so kindly she asked if I needed anything else and I said a salad would be nice, then I got up without my coat and walked over to the salad bar. The cafeteria erupted into hysterics and some students pelted me with their buttered rolls. The girl was good-natured and accepted my apologies. Later I would use the incident in a psychology paper.

Monica was my closest friend ever, followed by my mom. One day when I was a little kid, about nine years old, it seemed to me that my mom was feeling down. Wanting to cheer her up I wrote her a poem.

END OF SEASON

When the leaves are dressed in scarlet gold,
This is the sign of autumn as we all know,

Next comes the howl of a north wind blow,

Then the trees and leaves are covered with snow.

By Christopher Hurtubise 1966

I pasted it on a piece of green construction paper, something else she kept till the end of her life and I found it after she died. In later years my mom and I would enjoy getting together for tea. Most of the time I drank Coke or beer.... Hmmm...Cokeahol! When I left Wyoming I packed up everything, being the pack rat that I am. When I lived in Eaton, New Hampshire my mom came to visit, and taking a small sip of tea she squinted her eyes and asked; "what is this, hay?". The tea was about six years old, and, evidently, didn't resemble tea much anymore. After that she would pull a bag of tea from some recess or pocket of hers and decline mine. My mom understood me extremely well and toward the end of her life she would expand on thoughts about things we had done, why we both acted the way we did, and gave me invaluable advice. Shortly before she died she made one last trip out of the home she had lovingly made. It was just three houses down to my apartment but it was a significant trip for her. The steps to the second floor were an ordeal for her. When at long last she sat down at the kitchen table I produced an unopened box of Salada Tea. Cellophane still wrapped tightly. Not a molecule of air capable of entering. No matter, she had her own. We had an incredible time together, never once did we mention the cancer that was feeding on her frail body. We focused on the memories we had. A few days later she told me, while sitting on the black leather couch in the living room, that she was too weak to go outside the house again. Knowing her love of frits (what she called French Fries), I went to the nearest McDonalds and got a large order of French Fries. She was able to eat one. One. I had to leave so she wouldn't see me cry. Oh Mom.

Back on the road with my trusty but mangled Yamaha I set my sites East. Lunch was at some Stuckey's, fit in while taking care of the bike. As the day progressed I felt good and was sure I'd make Albuquerque by early evening. The sun had just set and I was only about forty miles away. Sirens and flashing lights grabbed my attention as a state trooper quickly pulled up behind me. No waving him on. After pulling over I dismounted from the bike but left it idling. With my helmet off I went to the officers window and asked what the problem was. "Your tail light is out". As he finished the word 'out', the bike died. He asked if I wanted him to stay while I tried to figure out the problem. A replacement bulb didn't help and now I couldn't start the bike. The fuse was fine. The temperature was dropping quickly and it was a desolate section of road. He said if I left the bike for help the bike would be stolen. That didn't leave many options. He was adamant that I not camp there as he didn't feel it was safe and he said the paperwork on a homicide was killer. Where was he in Utah? Then he asked me if I had ever 'hitched' a ride. "Hitched?" "All you do is hold onto the 'B' pillar of the car". He rolled down his front window and I was told to hold onto the pillar that separated the front from the rear window. His light bar was still on warp speed. Blinding. After I moved my bike so it was beside his squad car I got on the Yamaha and gripped the pillar as tightly as I could. Due to the accident in Utah, my grip was rather weak and I let go before we made it a quarter of a mile, just 19.75 miles to go. Unfazed he said I should just hold his hand. He grabbed his steering wheel with his right hand

and extended his left arm out the window. He didn't have hands, he had paws. Grizzly paws! It was like I was just a baby; his hands were enormous. With his bone-crushing grip in place, he started to take off. Slowly his left shoulder began to protrude out the window and then he let go. "Got any rope?"

The idea was to tie a rope to his rear bumper and to my handlebars. The only piece of rope I had was a little over six feet long. When he got out of the cruiser I was stunned. The guy must have been an easy 6'6", 300 plus pounds without an ounce of fat. No wonder his hands were huge, the rest of him was also! We tied the rope to his bumper and, not knowing better, tied the other end to my chrome handlebars. Normally when a vehicle is towed the towed vehicle acts as the brakes, this wasn't normal.

He got back in the cruiser and told me to hang on. For the next twenty miles his strobe bar was at full blast, though he did shut the siren off, and he cruised at a steady 55mph. In the beginning it wasn't too bad, almost fun. Then I noticed we had been going up a long hill and the crest was just ahead. On the way down the backside of the hill he maintained the speed limit of 55mph. Problem was the bike wanted to coast faster. There was about a scant eighteen inches between his bumper and my front tire. Ever so carefully I would apply a small amount of brake to the front wheel just before it would touch his bumper. The rope would snap tight and catapult me back toward the cruiser, and the scenario would repeat itself. It must have been some tough rope because I can't recall how many times I went through it. Why I don't have all gray hair is beyond me. At one point I tried just letting the Yamaha's front tire rub up against the rear bumper of the cruiser. Big mistake. The friction would make it so the wheel wanted to turn sideways and that would have made me lose control of the bike, and I had learned that motorcycle flying is a tough sport. At last I could make out the filling station he had talked about; it was on the opposite side of the interstate. The off ramp was a long 360-degree, angled exit ramp. Joy. The cruiser barely slowed for the off ramp. The angle of the bumper to my handlebars had the effect of trying to pull the bike down. Frantically I tried to untie the rope. Time was scarce. It seemed best that I should jump off the bike on the right side and attempt a shoulder roll. Just as I stood up and got ready to jump we exited the off ramp and had made it to the other side. The officer pulled the cruiser up to the stations worn garage doors then he got out to talk with the attendant. After I had untied the bike and calmed my nerves I went over to say thank you to the officer. He told me the attendant would give the Yamaha and me a ride to a bike shop in Albuquerque. The attendant and I talked for a while and he explained to me how the hood of the car near me had become crushed. Just the week prior Officer Friendly had stopped in for a coffee and was accosted by a tall drunk man. My friendly officer had taken enough abuse, reached out with one hand, grabbed the drunk by the scruff of his shirt, picked him up, then, all with using just one arm, slammed the drunk onto the hood of the car and told the drunk he owed the owner a new hood.

It was a couple of hours until the station closed and not a single car showed up for gas. When at last the attendant could leave we loaded the Yamaha into the back of his Ford truck and proceeded to go to Albuquerque. After a warm twenty-minute drive we arrived at a repair shop in an industrial part of town. Being too wound up to sleep, and honestly, afraid if I slept it would allow thugs to pummel me for sport, I stayed up all night until the shop opened. Took a long time before I heard 'The Crack of Dawn'. It wasn't the first all-nighter I pulled in college, but it was certainly the most unpleasant, as I was cold, lonely and frightened. Thoughts of the truck driver who had run me off the road and the employee who had set me up raced through my muddled mind.

Till now my mind had served me well. When I first entered high school I was a C student. By the time I left high school I was a bored 'A' student. College proved to be more of a challenge yet for some reason I tended to 'choke-up' on exams. The grades I got typically didn't reflect how well I understood the material. In the lab section of the courses I often excelled. Things in the lab situation often made more sense to me than the dry book material. Physics lab was a hoot for me; it explained so much. Microbiology was fascinating. Things seemed to be going so swell in a chemistry lab that the proctor allowed me to proceed at my own speed and soon I was several weeks ahead of the rest of the class. In the lab there were special hoods that allowed for the student to work in an environment where any fumes were pulled away. I liked the hood. One week I was given an unknown material and had to determine how much of a particular substance was in it. The fill-in proctor wasn't aware that I was several weeks ahead and gave me a sample intended for another experiment. When I mixed A with B there was a large explosion that knocked me violently backward into a counter and simultaneously released a large cloud of black poisonous smoke. The professor was called over and went over my notes and found the problem. He asked why I was working in the hood when the procedure I had been following didn't call for it. When I replied that I always felt safer in the hood he nodded his head. Then he explained that had I not been in the hood the fumes from my experiment would have killed all but those closest to the doors. Sometimes I think the only reason I graduated is that they wanted a safe way to get rid of me.

My mind works in an analytical way and some day I'll figure out how to profit from that. Years later in that fateful automobile accident my mind would literally be ripped, but till that time it worked flawlessly. Not saying I used it to the best of my ability, but it was a good mind. My mind tends to get me into trouble, as I tend to listen to it before I listen to my heart. A simple thing like a snowy December day would provide my mind with a reason to be outside.

It was a typical blustery snow filled day that Saturday when Ron and I thought it would be wise to walk a few miles to downtown and screw around. When we approached a traffic light on Forest Ave. I playfully pushed Ron into a snow bank for no reason other than it was fun. There had been no traffic till that point. Just as I pushed him over sideways a city bus drove over my footprints and disappeared into the white swirling cloud. Ron thought I had heard the bus, but I hadn't because the snow-covered street and the howling wind had kept either of us from hearing the approaching doom. For over two city blocks my footprints were covered over while Ron's were still there. Christ. Not being enough to deter us we kept on with our aimless quest. After a few hours we decided to head home and as we walked back up Congress St. we passed Portland City Hall. The majestic granite block building is built right up to the sidewalk so the small side street at the end isn't clearly visible until you pass City Hall. Again, for no apparent reason I thought what great fun to pull Ron back into a snow bank and fall on top of him. Just as I yanked on Ron's blue parka with the wolf fur trimmed hood and pulled him back a large city plow truck that was coming up the side street lost control and came across the sidewalk and sprayed us with snow. Had there not been that couple extra seconds we would have become kidsicles. A lot different scenario a decade or so later when three of us would nearly die on Devil's Tower.

Some say I had a death wish, but I think I was just young and reckless and while I didn't have a death wish, I didn't mind flirting with it either. The dorm had study rooms on some floors and when I didn't need absolute quiet I would use one of the three-sided rooms. Invariably we would horse around and once we noticed how the three part windows opened wide, with the center section stationary, and had no bars to keep an idiot from falling out. With the end window wide open I stuck my head out and gave a 'Yee-hah', then heard someone above me. She was well endowed and called for me to look up, and when I did she took her top off, jiggled her breasts and asked; "How do you like my brains?" It is probably how she got through school. Looking back out I noticed the wide window had about a four-inch ledge. With my study partner still at the table I climbed out onto the narrow ledge yelling, "I can't take it any more". He knew I was joking, but he was alarmed by the situation and called for me to come inside, which didn't deter me. With careful legwork I made it across the wide expanse, eight stories high, with little to hold onto, then knocked on the closed window at the other end for him to let me in. He thought I was nuts and this event was funny until a few weeks later a girl in the dorm opposite truly couldn't take it anymore and jumped to her death.

Day Seven

While leaning against the bike I watched the sun slowly rise. An hour later and the repair shop was open and toasty warm. The mechanics were very accommodating and fit me right in. About two hours later I was on the road. The problem with the bike stemmed from the first accident in Utah, some wire had been yanked tight when the bike flipped and the protective covering had worn off, causing the bike to short out and stall.

Reflecting back I realize that my brain has, on occasion, also shorted out and stalled. During my sophomore we had a 'rush' party at the fraternity. It was January, start of the spring semester. It was a typical party with lots of beer, loud music, and as many sorority girls as we could coax over. The idea was to show some freshmen a good time and try to get new members for the fraternity. During the party someone suggested we go to a small, closed, ski area outside of town for a tubing party the next day. We brought wine, cheese, crackers, inner tubes, and of course, sorority girls. It had been difficult but I had managed to convince a couple of the freshmen from the previous nights party to attend. Jim had been a hard sell on the idea as he needed to study, but I suggested that he not drink at the ski area, just try out tubing. With Jim I had felt a connection and thought he'd be a great asset to the house, plus tubing is wicked fun!

One of the fraternity brothers lived at the defunct ski area and took care of the property. He was able to get the rope tow running so we wouldn't have to hoof it up the hill with the bulky inner tubes. Things were going well and Jim and his friends were having a blast. As I rested at one of the rotting picnic tables I watched Jim take a fast ride down the hill. He was face down and gripping the inner tube with all his might when he hit a large mogul and became airborne. In mid-flight he lost his grip on the tube and with an audible thud he landed chest first on the peak of the next mogul. It was immediately obvious he was seriously injured. Several of us rushed over to help as he struggled to get up. We carried him to one of the better picnic tables and laid him down on his back. He was gasping for air and with a weak voice telling us he needed help breathing. It was a desperate situation and a call for help was placed, but we all knew it would take a half hour for an ambulance to reach us. I volunteered to give him mouth-to-mouth respiration, but one of the older fraternity brothers said it would only make things worse. From the start of the accident I felt responsible, why had I pressured him into this? He was in agonizing pain and the ambulance was taking forever. As the Chrysler had a massive back seat I suggested we put him in the back and I'd drive him back to Laramie. Again I was voted down. Precious minutes ticked by and finally the ambulance arrived and whisked Jim away. Not being able to stay behind, I followed the ambulance back to town. Twice during the descent from Lincoln Memorial down treacherous I-80 the ambulance stopped. I would pull over and wait. The hospital personnel wouldn't allow me inside, as I wasn't family. His family lived in Schenectady, NY, thousands of miles away. A doctor told me to go home and call to check on his condition. Every five minutes I'd call and every five minutes I'd be told they couldn't release information, as I wasn't a family member. Finally I was asked if I knew how to reach his family so I told the doctor that I could get their phone number. The doctor asked what my relationship with Jim was and I described how we met and how I had persuaded him to join the tubing party. Jim was D.O.A. Guilt and sorrow cursed through my body and I felt physically ill. What had I done? The following day there was a small article in the school paper then no further mention of Jim.

While I can still picture Jim, drinking a beer and laughing, in the hallway of the house, my mind has shorted out and erased his last name. Several times over the following years I would try to find the article and get in contact with his family. How they must hate me. Part of me believes that if I really wanted to I could contact his folks but I think that I am simply too afraid to do it.

It's about six hundred miles to Laramie from the motorcycle shop. A full day's ride. For the beginning of November the weather was grand. More sun and warmth. Personally I enjoy both warm and cold weather. In high school I started hiking in the White Mountains in New Hampshire. This is where Mt. Washington is located, home of the highest recorded land wind speed of 231 mph. Winds are stronger than hurricane force for almost one third of the year. A lot of people have died on Mt Washington because they were not prepared for the ferocious winds and climate. At only 6,288 feet above sea level it is actually lower than Laramie, Wyoming. The University of Wyoming is the highest learning institute in America, 7200 feet above sea level. What makes Mt. Washington and the surrounding area special is the lay of the land and how different wind currents collide there. This is probably what attracted a group of us in high school to climb there. During senior year a group of four of us headed to a smaller mountain for a day trip. Trip is the operative word. The boots I had were too flexible and the guy at the climbing shop wouldn't rent crampons to me since I had 'Mickey Mouse' boots; boots that aren't stiff enough for crampons to stay on. That certainly wasn't enough to deter us, so off we went. Things went rather well right up to the summit. We were commenting on how small the trees were at the top when I went over to check one out. Turns out the trees were standard height pine trees; there was just a helluva mound of snow. So when I stepped near the scrub I fell down along side the tree right up to my armpits. My nice new dark green wool pants that Monica had gotten me for Christmas were torn from ankle to butt. Chilly. Shrinkage. For the way down we were more cautious of the cursed crippled pines. As we were traversing a small 100-foot ice covered cliff, Steve, directly behind me, said, "Wow, what a place to fall". As if on cue as he uttered the word 'fall', I slipped and fell off the cliff. Instinct took over and though I had never used an ice axe before I slammed the pick into the ice and self arrested with my body hanging over the edge.

Another time Steve and I had wanted to go cross-country skiing and do some ice-skating at the same time. We went to Riverside Golf Course, which provided a nice mix of hills and flat terrain and had the bonus feature of a pond on the backside. After experimenting with small ski jumps (rather tough with cross country skis) we headed over to the pond. The ice was cleared of snow from the steady wind in the area. As we skated around one area Steve mentioned that the ice felt thin to him and we should probably leave. "No, it feels fine to me" I proclaimed just as I broke through the ice and fell into the pond. Again the act of spreading my arms out wide saved my butt, as I kept myself from submerging in the chilly water. Soaking wet, I changed back into my ski boots and headed back to the car. Steve laughed the whole way back. We returned the next week but brought Jerry and his toboggan with us. At the end of the day Steve and I had loaded our gear back into his parent's white Ford station wagon. Jerry wanted one last ride. He jumped on at the hill right above the parking lot and had planned to slide right up beside the wagon. Steering on a toboggan isn't the most accurate thing in the world and he got a little off course and also went a little faster than he had expected. He hit the snow bank to our right and became airborne, like motorcycle flying landing is always the tough part. The hood of the green Valiant next to us provided Jerry with a landing strip and he hit it with a loud thud then proceed to ride the toboggan right over the hood, windshield, roof, and the off the back of the car. Steve and I were fit to be tied but the elderly couple in the Valiant was still screaming as Jerry quickly loaded the toboggan.

Not wanting to stall my trip any further, I headed up through beautiful New Mexico and into Colorado. The roads had little traffic and riding was a joy again. It was pretty much an uneventful day. The only problem was I was running late due to the repairs. While driving through the Denver area traffic picked up considerably. A police car had been in the left lane beside me and was staying in my blind spot. In a heartbeat the sirens wailed and the lights flashed then they went off. A booming voice over a loud speaker announced; "You on the motorcycle, you have a tail light out and you must pull over at the next exit for a repair". After I gave a thumb up sign and nodded in their direction the troopers sped off ahead of me. Being cash strapped I was hoping for an easy fix. Thankfully it was just a bulb. Within minutes I was back on the road headed toward wonderful Wyoming. Risking the chance of meeting yet another officer of the law I sped up as I was ready to say hello to my old bed. The drive from Denver to Fort Collins is a bit boring, but the drive from Fort Collins to Laramie is fun with hills, interesting terrain, and wide-open pedal to the metal straight driving. The area around the Colorado-Wyoming border intrigues me to this day. It is rugged and wind blown.

Desolate. I can picture myself in a log cabin being content.

My first year in Wyoming was tough. Being so far away from home, everything so different. As time went by I began to appreciate the wide-open feel. It was not uncommon to see antelope running with their gracious stride beside the highway. Breath taking. They tasted good too. Once, when going to Seminoe Reservoir to see the Maxson's I had to stop the Chrysler 300. A huge herd of antelope was crossing the dusty road. As they raced around either side of the car I actually gasped as one bounded over the hood of my father's car. How could you not love this land?

My freshman year I joined the Kappa Sigma fraternity. It was housed in a majestic stone building at the beginning of fraternity row. We actually paid attention to grades while we consumed massive amounts of beer. Practical jokes are a part of life in a frat house. Sometimes they were aimed at sororities, or more commonly, at other fraternities. Sigma Nu was our neighbor and they were known for being a bit stuffy. Thinking of that made a group of us wonder how to play a joke on them dealing with 'stuffy'. A big ole jackrabbit from Vedauwoo proved to be the bait. The poor bunny had met an untimely death after being introduced to someone's car. It was up to a group of us pledges to get the bunny into the chimney of the Sigma NU house. Four of us climbed onto the roof while they were having dinner. Nice romantic fire burning. Perfect timing. We dropped Mr. Bunny and could hear him slide part way down. Rigor mortis had yet set in. Giggling like a cackle of high school girls we found our way off the roof. Sigma Nu has nice panoramic windows in front, so we parked ourselves across the street. Soon the house was filled with smoke. Not known if barbecue bunny was ever served.

Often I was the recipient of a practical joke. That was fine, as I lived by the motto; "don't get mad, get even". I'd get even in spades. The memory cells that should remind me of what my roommate Chris did to receive his joke has long since died. Chris had a special relationship with his thin golden hair. He would use his electric razor to keep it trimmed. In the amount of time it took him to dry and prettify his hair, I could take a shower, dry off, get dressed, and head off to class. Something had to be done. With help from another fraternity brother we got hold of his shampoo bottle. As synthetic oil was not yet available, we had to make do with nice, sweet Castrol 10W-40 oil. We replaced about two-thirds of the shampoo with the motor oil. Till now, I have always disavowed any knowledge of the incident.

He may have been behind the time I was covered with snow while taking a shower. Or the time my clothes were hidden, or a multiple of other incidents. That was fine, I was prepared. After I became in charge of the kitchen the number of incidents against me dropped dramatically. This may due to the rumor that Ex-Lax may be in the pudding, or, perhaps chopped, raw liver. One of my favorite tricks was to apply just a drop of super glue to a water glass at dinnertime. The brothers were creatures of habit and tended to sit in the same place night after night. One small drop of super glue was just enough to add resistance to the full glass of water. The recipient would go for the water, encounter resistance and, without thought, pull harder. The water glass would fly off the table and soak the poor soul. Everyone loved that one.

Mark thought it would be funny to hit me with a water balloon when I got back from class. Ha Ha. The following day I was perched on the roof to the front door entryway, water hose in hand. Does his mother know what comes out of his mouth?

Every time I returned home for Christmas vacation my Dad would quiz me on all things Wyoming. He would track my movements across the land and know amazingly well where I would be, when I ought to be home. Some of this may be attributed to his extensive driving. During WWII he was the lead driver for a contingent of fuel tankers known as the Red Ball Express. He and his buddies drove throughout Europe in door less trucks, quicker to jump out when shot at, delivering fuel to the front line. Throughout the six years I attended the University not once did my Dad not know when it was me that was calling. Long before Caller ID, if the phone rang he would say, "That's Chris". It always befuddled my Mom, especially since I didn't have any particular set time to call, and she thought a mother's intuition would be stronger than my father's physic ability.

Returning home for Christmas could be a shock. There would be times when the age of my parents would startle me. Other times it would all be quite amusing. My first Christmas back it was just my folks and I opening our presents, as my siblings would be over later. The gifts were always modest but heartfelt. After we had exchanged gifts my Dad brought out an extra box for me. Inside was a thick, black vintage Harley Davidson belt. It was the belt my Dad used after he returned from the war. It was also the belt he used to spank us boys with. "This is the belt you use to beat me with!" "What? I never beat you boys!" Selective memory. Soon Leo showed up and exclaimed, "Wow, that's the belt you use to beat us with!" "I never beat you boys!" Not much later my other brother showed up and exclaimed the same and received the same response. Finally Monica showed up and as soon as she saw the heavy belt she exclaimed; "Wow, that's the belt you use to beat the boys with" At that point our Dad sunk into his black leather chair, pipe in hand, and said that it was amazing how all of his children have warped memories.

It would be in the following year, when I was losing my vision, that this stretch of road would prove daunting. As my eyesight got dramatically worse day-to-day it was this drive that would be my final drive that semester. Earlier, while studying in the basement science library I noticed that I was getting headaches and having trouble reading the large clock. At first I wrote it off to eyestrain and didn't pay it much attention. Soon I needed new glasses and when they arrived in two weeks it seemed they must have got the prescription wrong. The optometrist was stunned, and he sent me to an ophthalmologist, my eyes had gotten worse in a mere two weeks. Two weeks later I had another new pair of eyeglasses, and again, no real improvement. At this point I started seeing the doctor two to three times a week. My eyes were deteriorating at an amazing speed. The blackboard had become a struggle to read, even from the front row; at times I would see two clocks in the library where I knew only one

existed. After leaving my girlfriend's home that winter day, I found I could no longer read the highway signs, even with my brand-new glasses. As I approached each sign I would pull over, get out of the car, walk up to the sign and read it. Just the day before it wasn't a problem. Now the wind and snow that I loved before proved to be a significant adversary. The weather conditions made it difficult to read the signs, even when I was directly below them. On the stretch of road that I had grown to love, I could no longer find the pavement. Not owning the

Chrysler 300, I was driving a 1968 pale blue Volkswagen square back. Off road. Seeing a set of lights I aimed for them and found my way back to the road and Laramie, parked the car, and flunked out of college, unable to read the exam. My eyes stabilized as quickly as they had gone AWOL. With yet another pair of new glasses I able to return to school the following semester, but I would have a heavy work load, as I had to repeat several courses.

The night air was cold and crisp, like lettuce should be. Having made it to the border I pushed the Yamaha even harder. Like the beginning of the trip this section of highway was desolate. Don't remember seeing another vehicle for the last thirty miles. The vast darkness of the night was relaxing. Stars brightly lit. Peace. Its engine humming smoothly, no electrical problems, the bike and I were finally back to Zen. The final part of the journey was exhilarating. Speed, cold, home.

This was freedom. To be free, not simply in the literal sense, but to feel freedom course through your veins like a shot of whiskey in your gut, is exhilarating. It made me think of the hovel of an apartment we had rented in Rawlins while we worked in the treacherous oil fields. Only a couple blocks away was the gothic state penitentiary. A beautiful building to look at: but only from the outside. Every day when we returned home from work we drive along two sides of it in our one ton four door pickup. One particular Friday evening we were all wound a bit tight and were feeling frisky. The truck, while less than a year old, was showing its age due to the abuse it took on a daily basis. It had a manual choke, which was uncommon even then. As we were driving down the hill, with the prison on our right, we noticed that a baseball game was being played between the prisoners and guards. The small grandstand was filled to capacity and we had never seen so many inmates out on the grounds at one time. Our driver asked us if we were ready for some fun, and of course we were. He pulled the choke and let of the gas then accelerated, causing the truck to emit a hellacious backfire. Nothing other than the real thing could sound so much like substantial gunfire. Everyone on the field dropped to the ground, while the spectators in the grandstand either jumped off or lay down upon each other. Guards were at full alert and not a soul on the prison grounds moved an iota. While we had a grand laugh, we knew better than to drive along side the front and expose ourselves as the guilty party. From that point on we took a different way home.

The fraternity house was truly a home away from home, and I am grateful that it was there. Pity that time was not kind to it and fraternities have become less popular. The forced interaction with other students helped us all prepare for 'The Real World'. When Christmas arrived I was all over it, putting up lights from stem to stern and making the house a home. Sophomore year a group of us went into the woods, thirty miles away, to cut a massive pine tree down to use as our Christmas tree. Once fallen, we couldn't budge it. Someone had a climbing rope and we used that to pull it out. The thing about climbing ropes is that they are designed to stretch, so if a climber falls there is some give in the line, otherwise you could use steel cable. Being naïve to the manufacturing methods of the rope a group of us stood by and watched as the truck pulled the rope taunt. The noise a snapped rope makes is unmistakable, getting hit in the back with it was yet another lesson in being airborne. The guy on the other side wasn't as lucky as I, for I just landed in a pile of fluffy water crystals while he got hit in an ear and lost his hearing for several months.

My attention to the house, and its members didn't go unnoticed. Freshman year I was elected Pledge of the Year. The presentation was held in a hotel in Colorado, where we could party all night and not worry about driving. The traditional way to present the award is to give the honoree a pledge paddle, but to also give two hearty swats to his butt first. As I had heard rumors that I may win, I had placed a towel in my pants to lessen the blow, should I win. Up on stage I was asked to bend over and grab my ankles, and in front of everyone the fraternity brother reached into my pants and pulled out the towel. The swats were hard, but (no pun there either) it was all in good fun. A couple years later I would be elected Man of the Year, and my first duty was to announce Pledge of the Year and give the two swats. The second swat nearly lifted the poor fellow off the floor. My final semester was spent in Fort Collins, Colorado, where I did my pharmacy internship. Technically, at that point I was considered an alumnus, and was honored with Alumni of the Year shortly before I graduated.

At the frat house, all bright and warm, I found Pete. We would share future adventures that would test our survival skills, then later in life our paths would go separate ways. At the time though he was cramming for an exam and I was exhausted. I would talk with him later. At home Ray was out so I took my first shower in days and crawled into bed.

The following day I was back in class. All my fellow pharmacy students were talking about their drug trip. The bus ride was incredible, I was told. "So Clay, what did you do with your week off?"
"Nothing much, went on a bike trip".

Author's Notes

Throughout Drug Trip you'll notice a few different writing styles. The main story is how I currently write, and think – as warped as that may be. If an older piece of work is used I insert the piece just as it was written, without updating. The poem 'Missing' is an example.

'Missing' was written the first night I spent at Jerry's place in Rawlins Wyoming. As I lay on the couch I grabbed a piece of lined paper and wrote the poem, which I then included with a letter to my Mom. It was a difficult night for me. I had no money, no job prospects, and a growling stomach. When I get in such situations I focus on the next day. In the third book of this trilogy this method of getting through a tough time became crucial, as I recuperated from a head injury. The difference is in the second and third book sometimes I focused on the next ten minutes. When ten minutes would pass I would focus on the next ten minutes, and so on.

The poem 'I Lost My Sister' was written after I returned to Portland. Monica had died in my arms just hours earlier. No one could solace me and I couldn't sleep until I had written the poem. Granted, it could use some editing, but I leave it as it was written at the time. In book two, Dog Trip, my best friend Mark dies tragically. I went on a high-speed drive through some of Mark and my favorite mountain areas. At about 2:00 AM I pull over near the now fallen Old Man of the Mountain in New Hampshire and wrote on a paper bag a poem for Mark. His father kept the poem till he also died years later.

'Mom's Story' was written as a request from a friend who knew my Mom's history. At the time I wanted to keep the story short and to the point. A lot of people have asked me to expand on it, and I may do so in the future. In book three I include 'Monica'. The story was difficult to write and I include it as it was originally written. People are surprised that I include humor in a story such as 'Monica', but if you look closely you'll find some form of humor in most any story.

'End of Season', well, what can I say? At the time I was nine years old! My Mom loved it and held onto it for the rest of her life.

My Drug Trip

Transportation

Supplies Needed

Where to Wander

Camping Supplies

State of Mind

People I've Met

What Was That I Ate?

Shaman: Devil's Deal

Clay Hurtubise

Dear Readers,
On the following pages is an early draft of the first chapter of my next book. It is due out in late 2009/early 2010.

Shaman: Devil's Deal, is the story of a young Shaman growing up during a tumultuous time. His family threatened and then attacked, he must learn the ways of his forefathers in order to survive. He works with his extended family to gain strength and to overcome the wicked ways of those who have chosen a different path.

All Artwork is by Lars Christensen.

CHAPTER ONE
Elementary

H e was always good with his hands. He could fix most anything with just a few simple tools. When his father, the
Shaman, died, he fixed that too.

My grandfather was three quarter Native American Indian; only
God knows what the other quarter was. I doubt it was human.
He had a way about him that is hard to describe: dignified,
never condescending, a twinkle in his dark brown eyes, and a
patience that seemed unnatural. Often he would take my hand
and hold it firmly while he explained how something worked;
could be a motor, how the tides flowed, or how to think five
moves ahead in chess. When he held me, it was not like a typical
parental feeling, more like a mild electric current. After a certain
point he would break the bond and I would feel both more
assured about life, and also tired like I had spent the day out in
the sun, a good tired.

My burly Father was mostly absent from my early life; he was
too busy supporting the local bar. Not one to get inebriated, he
simply enjoyed the atmosphere of the smoky pub over that of a
loving home. Dad had never abused me or subjected me to hor-

rible things; mostly his abuse was simply not being there. Though if I ever needed him I always knew where I could find him: and he would proudly pick me up and spin me around while announcing to the other patrons; "Isn't he a fine young buck?" Dad was also gifted, but chose not to pursue it: at least not yet. Work was simply another four-letter word to him. When Father held me, it was like a lesser Grandfather: still felt something special, but not to the same magnitude.

My grandfather had built our simple wooden framed home on an idyllic five acre lot. Most of the fertile land had been cleared for farming, but along the river stood tall Weeping Willows and majestic Oak trees. It had taken him years to complete the structure, while other homes were designed and built in a much shorter time period. It wasn't a large house, but the attention to detail was amazing. He incorporated shelves under the stairs, deep windowsills that served as benches, and a simple yet charming molding that wound it's way from room to room without a visible seam. The stone fireplace was large and in the chimney he had incorporated serpentine air chambers to trap heat. All the stones were from our fields and it was truly a 'fieldstone' fireplace. It was a home of warmth. Guests always remarked how much better they felt both physically and emotionally after their stay.

Our main pet was Silk, a tough, pretty, and loving Soft Coated Wheaton Terrier. When I was in fifth grade, and Kye in fourth, we spent one night under the stars: we spread blankets over a patch of the trodden corn field, built a small fire, and told ghost stories till we both fell asleep. When we awoke there was a small puppy curled tightly between us, all snuggled up in the blankets. Kye said her fur was the same color as the corn silk, thus her name. She was our protector from day one; she made it her duty that no harm would come down upon us without her putting up a ferocious fight first. While she rarely barked, her deep, low growl tipped us off of danger more than once.

As a puppy, Silk was a hellion. She pooped, peed, barfed and created havoc in every corner of our once peaceful home. Mother was about to become unglued. It took a lot to unnerve Mother. She was graceful but not snobby, caring and helpful yet made sure you learned how to take care of yourself and your family. She was not one to yell, so when she lowered her voice and called your name you knew you had some explaining to do. More than once she asked how we came to find Silk, and our story never changed. Grandfather never asked, but he always had an ear bent toward our discussion on how we came about finding Silk. After six months or so Silk started to quiet down and finally learned that home wasn't a bathroom. She no longer chewed things that aught not be chewed. Her favorite toy became old tied up wool socks. She would carry them around the house and fall asleep with the worn socks tucked under her furry chin. Her intelligence was surprising and she sensed how I felt: if I were sad or angry, she would reach out and put her paw on my forearm, then give me a quick lick. It was hard to stay mad with Silk around. The oddest thing was that when Silk put her paw on me when I was upset, it almost felt like Grandfather's hand: that mild current and feeling assured, then tired.

135

Occasionally Silk would give chase to one of our cats, but she would never back them into a corner. If anything, she was like a thirty pound, furry police dog: if a fight broke out, she would break it up – no animal ever fought back to Silk. She protected the whole family, though I could tell I was her favorite. If Silk sensed danger she would sit between my legs and let anyone or anything know she meant business. She wasn't always all business though, she enjoyed her games: flying squirrel was her favorite. Either Kye or I would sit on the couch and have the coffee table in front of the couch cleared off, and then Silk would be held back away from the furniture while the person on the couch Held up a toy. On 'launch', Silk would be released and she would charge up to the coffee table, jump onto it, then launch herself airborne. She would get so much height sometimes she would almost sail pass over our heads.

While Kye and I would explore the mountain-lined valley, Silk was always by our side. The valley our tribe shared with Mother Nature was about six by thirteen miles and filled with wildlife. We had been there for generations, tending the land while the land provided for us all. Our home was near a steep cliff, and that is where the cave was. Someday I would explore the cave near Grandfather's workshop, but not now.

Our friends, especially Hoice and his sister, Elizabeth, would explore with us. On the other side of town there was one dark home we always kept our distance from: it wasn't that it was scary, but that we all felt an unwelcome presence there. The only time I saw anyone there was during a humid summer day long ago. Our little gang was kicking and passing a soccer ball down Valley Street when the ball landed against the unpainted picket fence. Tall scrubs grew on the other side of the fence so the view of the home was obscured. Just as I ran up to retrieve the ball, a hand reached out and grabbed the fence. A hand with a tattoo: one I would see again. After a few quick strides, I turned to look back at the eerie house. There were no remnants of the mysterious hand, but in front of the weathered picket fence gate stood a tall, young girl, waving at me. She had dark, long hair and her physique was stunning. Something about her alarmed me: something deep inside warned me to beware. Later I would see her again, and as time passed our chance encounters would increase: always making me uneasy though she was always friendly. Her name, I learned, was Aoife: an old Irish name for an evil young girl. Ironically, in the story Aoife was turned into a crow, and the related raven was a sacred bird to us.

Hoice wasn't athletic like Kye, so Hoice tended to hang out with me more often than with Kye. Elizabeth wasn't a particularly attractive child, but Kye and I liked her robust personality, and we both enjoyed her company. Hoice and Elizabeth fought like typical brother and sister, but when push came to shove they helped and protected each other. If it was mechanical, Elizabeth could fix it. We teased her and called her a tomboy, but she was all girl: just a girl that liked all things mechanical. Hoice was fascinated with photography and took his Brownie with him everywhere. As he had to pay for his own film, he learned how to develop and print his own black and white prints. He would have made Ansel Adams proud. Hoice and

Elizabeth lived in a modest home by the river that meandered to the far side of the valley. Often we would meet somewhere in the middle, often near the old town post office. Hoice was also interested in astronomy, and he set his camera up with a telescope to make some interesting pictures. The four of us grew up together but they had to move from the valley while we were in junior high school.

While we ventured all around the magical valley, only one place was off limits: that dark cave with a small entrance near grandfather's shop. Kye and I often thought about going in, and finally one night we gathered our courage and set out to explore. Heavy brush obscured the trail and the weather was quickly changing. A storm was brewing and the air electrified. When we found the entrance, Silk was there. Thinking she was there to play guard dog, we approached her quickly. She snarled. We were stunned, she had never snarled at us. We called her name, but she wouldn't move. The wind was now whip-

ping the low hanging branches whipping against us, and the rain had started with an intensity we had rarely witnessed. It wasn't hard to convince each other that this had been a bad idea. As soon as we turned our back to the cave, Silk was beside us acting perfectly normal.

We were allowed into grandfather's old workshop. It always looked the same: busy, not cluttered, and worn but not falling apart. It had a packed dirt floor, which gave it a musty smell, especially if the rains had been heavy. The exterior was clad in worn barn board that had turned dark grey with age. Sections of it curled and other parts showed splits in the wood. The bottom edge was like that of an old, frequently opened gate: the edges were rounded and smooth. While it looked like a faint breeze may blow it away, it stood the test of time and never even leaked a drop. The inside walls were covered partially with a honey yellow bead board that went about six feet high: above that the boards changed direction and were like the exterior wood. At first glance the shop seemed small when viewed from the main house, but to us, especially as little kids, the inside was cavernous.

Kye and I went to the older school on the edge of town, where the river cascaded over the rocks in a wondrous waterfall. We never really understood why our parents had us hoof all the way to that school, when a newer, larger school was closer. They would say it was more traditional, but we thought it was because that is where they had met. It was difficult to make friends there as all the other kids lived miles from our home. Kye was so athletic that he joined the basketball and football team of the other school, as our school didn't have much in the way of sports. That gave us an excuse to visit the new school, and it is where we made lasting friendships. We were both smitten with the same girl, but neither of us wanted to date her: we enjoyed her company like that of family. Her name was Acinom (Ack-in-om), but she preferred to be called Nom. Whenever the three of us were together, we explored, played games, and did typical kid stuff. While she was my age, she had a younger, rambunctious brother, Taes, who was a year younger than Kye. Taes and Kye were always trying to prove who was stronger, faster, or smarter. They never stopped competing, but as soon as the event was over, it was forgotten. The feeling I got from Taes was different than that from Nom. It wasn't a boy versus girl feeling, it was something deeper within me. Taes would become a great friend, but Nom was closer, more intimate without actually being near. Nom and I, or Kye and Nom, for that matter, never dated. Hoice and Nom went out 'as friends' a few times, but Nom was much more mature than Hoice.

Nom was Indian like my brother and I, while Taes was anyone's guess. They were brother and sister but Taes was adopted. Nom read extensively about Shamans and her other main interest was in animals: she envisioned using the two interests together and knew she would eventually become a veterinarian.   Her way with pets was magical and while only in the sixth grade she started a small home obedience school where she trained the masters more than the pets. Folks liked her way with animals and would often bring their critters to her house at all hours of the day. Often she had to turn them away, as she was simply too young and inexperienced to treat the animal. To watch her was an event in and of itself: the previously frantic animal would become calm in her presence. She would say soothing words and sounds to the animal; neither Kye, Taes, or myself ever understood a word of it, and when we asked her about what she was saying she would reply that she was simply comforting the animal. We all knew better. The odd thing was, though she could comfort and tend to wounds. If it was a small animal I simply held the animal firmly and the wounds seemed to heal faster.

Late one warm October afternoon we received a letter from the government. Not only did we have to vacate our land, but also the cemetery would have to be moved. Grandfather got very silent. Days went bye before he finally spoke; "I will move him". There wasn't any argument or discussion, nor did anyone ask how or offer any help. It was understood that grandfather would break the sacred soil over his father's holy resting site. When the time came, he woke me from a deep sleep. His warm leathery hand covered my mouth so I wouldn't alert the others. He could say so much with his eyes.

We met in front of his work shop, the bare single bulb swaying in the gentle breeze cast eerie shadows over the worn interior. With just a single shovel and an old dark green army duffle bag, we went out to the grave. Silk kept guard. Not knowing better, I simply started digging as soon as we arrived and it was one of the few times my grandfather ever hit me. Standing over me, he started to chant, slow and barely audible at first. Over the course of half an hour the pitch and frequency escalated until he was bellowing out words I had never heard: nor would I for quite some time.

Bones do rattle in a bag, and I found it both fascinating and creepy. We finished back where we had started, at the workshop. We had five weeks left at our old homestead, and then we were to move into the big, dark, forbidding city. The bright open sky, the animals moving in sync, and all we held dear were to be submerged permanently under water so cotton could be grown where it shouldn't. Against the towns' wishes, a large damn was to be built at the site of the waterfall. It seemed a 'done deal' from the beginning and no one, least those talking, understood why. During that dreadful five weeks we rarely laid eyes upon grandfather; though we heard a lot of chanting emanating from the workshop. On the last day, grandfather emerged from his intimate shop and held up for all to see the most wondrous site. A relief, all in an albino white material, of the surrounding land our family had lived with for generations. It wasn't particularly large, but extremely detailed. As a family we all knew what it was created from, which made it all the more fascinating. There were no seams, no joints. It appeared to be carved from a single piece of rock. As he emerged from the workshop, a sparkle caught my eye: it was something small hanging by a thread near the pull chain for the overhead light. Grandfather, normally impeccably dressed, had his shirttails hanging out and either the top button was undone or it had fallen off.

Word spread quickly though the reservation: there was something special at the Shaman's homestead. Though I was young, I will always remember him, the tall thin stranger with the tattoo on his hand. Somehow familiar, but at the time I couldn't place it. Silk had announced his arrival with her low throaty growl, barely audible to most. He was only a stranger to me, but obviously an unwelcome guest to grandfather. Stranger first tried to buy, then steal the sculpture. Dad fired a relic of a pistol into the air and Silk charged the man but he quickly fled. We would move to the city, away from the stranger, for now.

It was a massive state project to create the damn, and while it would be years before the valley was actually flooded, we were not allowed back onto our property. None of the project made sense, and it was difficult to find who was sponsoring the construction. Our tribe, together for generations, had to split up and leave our sacred land. When we left, never did any of us ever imagine we would see any part of it again. If only we had known.